The Historic
PARKS AND GARDENS
of Leicestershire and Rutland

Leonard Cantor and Anthony Squires

Kairos Press
Newtown Linford
Leicestershire
1997

Design and Layout by Robin Stevenson, Kairos Press
Body text in Century Schoolbook BT 10.5pt
Imagesetting by CDS Imaging, Leicester
Printed in Great Britain by Norwood Press, Anstey, Leicester.

Front cover: Staunton Harold Park, from the Lount–Melborne Road.
Back cover: Painting of Quenby Hall and Park, c.1740s. (artist umknown)

Kairos Press
552 Bradgate Road
Newtown Linford
Leicester LE6 0HB

Contents

List of Figures

ACKNOWLEDGEMENTS

A number of people have helped us to write this book. We are particularly grateful to Robert F. Hartley, Curator of Market Harborough Museum, for allowing us to reproduce a number of the excellent maps which he prepared for his most informative unpublished archeological survey, "The Formal Gardens of Leicestershire and Rutland" (1988). He also most kindly permitted us to draw upon this text, upon several of his other authoritative works and on his unrivalled knowledge of archaeological and historical aspects of the landscapes of Leicestershire and Rutland. Others who have helped us include Dr Christopher Brooke of the Leicestershire County Council Historic Buildings Conservation Team Staff; Dr Judith Roberts of the Centre for Conservation Studies at de Montfort University; Peter Liddle, Chief Archaeologist to Leicestershire County Council; John Ward for reading the text and making helpful comments; the County Archivist and his staff of the Leicestershire Record Office for granting us permission to reproduce some items in their care; the many landowners who over many years have allowed us access to their properties for the purpose of research and our publisher Robin Stevenson of Kairos Press for his support, enthusiasm and technological expertise.

Illustration Credits

The authors have pleasure in acknowledging the following for use of their copyright material:

The Duke of Rutland: fig. 49.

The Squire de Lisle: fig. 52 & back cover.

Robert F Hartley: figs. 9, 14, 15, 18, 20, 30, 31, 38, 40, 4246, 51, 56.

The Leicestershire Record Office and Local Studies Library: figs. 27, 43, 61.

The following are from Volume 4 Part 2 of Nichols: fig. 19 (Nichols p.430), fig. 22 (Nichols p.632), fig. 34 (Nichols p.647), fig. 39 (Nichols p.460)

English Heritage, for the maps in figs. 37 and 66.

The front cover, along with the maps and tables, are by Robin Stevenson of Kairos Press.

All other illustrations are by the authors.

INTRODUCTION

*T*he parks and gardens of England are among its greatest glories and probably no other country in the world has so rich and varied an inheritance of them. The two counties of Leicestershire and Rutland are no exception and although they are not renowned for famous parks and gardens and for the most part lack the sort of documentary evidence available in some counties to reconstruct their detailed histories, nonetheless they contain much to delight us.

Just how to define separately the terms "park" and "garden" is no easy matter; indeed, as is clear from the titles of many of the standard works on the subject they are often used synonymously. Suffice it to say that probably the simplest difference is one of scale: as defined in this book gardens are taken to be relatively small while parks are considerably larger. In the case of many stately homes, for example, they have, or have had, gardens immediately about the house, while their parks extend much further into the surrounding countryside. This book sets out to provide a guide to the history of the more important parks and gardens with which the two counties are, and have been endowed. In that respect it is neither a treatise on horticulture and gardening, nor does it deal with the gardens of 'ordinary' people.

During the two millennia in which parks have been carved out of the English countryside, and latterly inserted into English towns, they have taken different forms, reflecting different social and economic criteria. First introduced by the Normans, they were originally hunting parks devised to contain deer for their lordly owners to hunt. Unlike our modern conception of parks, they were generally well-wooded to provide "covert" for the deer and were surrounded by earthbanks and paling fences to contain them. In the later Middle Ages, as hunting became less practicable, though still wooded, they were replaced by "amenity" parks for the pleasure of their owners and to reflect their social status. Houses were built in them around which gardens were created. In the later seventeenth century, the fashion was for "formal" parks characterised, among other features, by long avenues of trees. A century later they were replaced by the sweeps of grassland, strategically placed trees and lakes associated with 'Capability' Brown which still provide the dominant image conjured up by most people when they think of a stately home set in its parkland. Clearly, the development of these parks and gardens can only be fully understood in relation to the houses they surrounded and the aspirations and fortunes of their owners; hence, in our book, we have included something of the men and women who made them.

Another type of park, the first to be widely open to the public, arrived in the latter half of the nineteenth century, namely the municipal or "people's" park, designed to provide some means of rest and relaxation for those living in the mushrooming Victorian towns. In our present century, many changes have taken place in our parks and gardens, as with virtually every other aspect of society. Many have been lost but much has been saved and, indeed, new ones taking new forms have been created and existing ones modified. Thanks to our increasing mobility and the willingness of owners to open their parks and gardens to the public, more people than ever before can appreciate and enjoy them. We hope that, in some measure, this small book will contribute to that appreciation and enjoyment.

Leonard Cantor
Anthony Squires
July 1997

1. *Loughborough from the north-west. This photograph was taken in 1979 before the later expansion of Loughborough University's campus, and the construction of the giant British Gas installation. The view includes the sites of five parks – Garendon Park (bottom left corner); Burleigh Park (centre-left, incorporating the triangular Holywell Wood); Loughborough Park (centre right, beyond the Nanpantan Road); Beaumanor Park (in the distance, top right); and Barrow Park (top left). On the right edge of the view is the still tree-covered site of the Domesday woodland of Loughborough known as 'The Outwoods'.*

CHAPTER ONE
Medieval Parks and Gardens, 1066 -1500

Very little is known of the parks and gardens of late eleventh century England although something of their occurrence and distribution is found in the scattered references in the Domesday Book of 1086. During the four and a half centuries from 1066 to about the year 1500, which for the purposes of this chapter comprise the Middle Ages, parks and gardens developed separately from one another, differing in both form and function. In early medieval times it was only the king and the richest nobles who set up parks for hunting and laid out gardens for vegetables, herbs, flowers and the benefits of gentle pleasures. Over the years both parks and gardens were to extend downwards through the social scale so that by the fourteenth century they might also be the property of the lesser nobility, knights of the shire and even the richer gentry.

Medieval Parks

Hunting parks were introduced into England by the Normans and by 1086 thirty-six of them, together with a number of hedged enclosures for deer called "hays", are recorded in the Domesday Book, though none are mentioned for Leicestershire or Rutland. The Normans, who were extremely fond of hunting, made their first major move towards the conservation and control of deer for this purpose by creating Royal Forests. Since, under the feudal system, the king owned everything and his nobles held their lands of him, successive monarchs graciously made grants to the higher nobles so they might set up hunting areas of their own. These were called Chases and were administered under the common law rather than the oppressive legislation governing the Royal Forests, which placed severe restrictions on those living in them . The distinctive Norman hunting park came into its own as the Royal Forests and Chases contracted and trees and deer became scarcer. In order to maintain a constant supply of game for hunting, animals were increasingly confined to carefully managed parks.

The Nature of the Parks

The medieval hunting park differed from our modern conception of a park in that it was usually well wooded in order to provide shelter for the deer. Typically, it occupied land on the edge of a lord's manor, distant from his dwelling, and where the soil was of inferior quality, the terrain unsuitable for agriculture and where woodland predominated. Along the perimeter of the chosen area a deep ditch was dug, the soil from this being thrown to the outside to form a continuous bank, about six feet or more high. On top of this a stout fence, usually of split oak pales, was erected. Ditch, bank and fence were known as the pale and formed a barrier to the attempted escape of the most determined deer. In some places stone walls replaced the fence and at *Lyddington*, in Rutland, for example, dead hedges were used, at least in part. Where the topography was suitable, no barrier was erected, as at *Groby* where a steep rock face was adopted. A lord frequently had considerable powers in dictating the line of the pale to suit his own convenience. At

Cadeby, for example, a parish boundary was realigned for this purpose, while at *Cold Overton* a change was made to the county boundary.

Not all the parks listed for Leicestershire and Rutland existed at the same time. The period during which most parks were created spanned the years 1200 to 1350. At all times parks were subject to change according to social and economic conditions and the wishes, fortunes and aspirations of their owners. The earliest known park was that at *Quorndon* which was established by Hugh, Earl of Chester, some time before 1135.[1] Another early creation was that at *Exton* in Rutland which is first recorded in 1185. The creation of a few parks can be dated with precision where a record of the agreement, or licence to empark has survived. At *Breedon*, for example, the park came into being when two local men agreed the emparment of the wood

2. *Cold Overton Park, Leicestershire, on the county boundary with Rutland. The wooded area to the right of the photograph marks the south-east part of the park (see p.14). The oval outline of the park, seen here as field boundaries, enclosed almost the maximum area of land with the minimum length of pale.*

on Cloud Hill. The text of this document is shown opposite.

The wood at *Launde* was emparked in 1248 following the partial deafforestation, (the formal abandonment of the Forest Laws) of the Forest of Rutland (Leighfield Forest). Here, the Prior obtained royal approval to enclose his wood and turn it into a park. *Flitteris Park*, in the royal manor of Oakham, came into being following the granting of a similar licence to Edmund, Earl of Cornwall, in 1250.

3. The quarry and remains of Buddon Wood at Quorn from the north-west. The medieval park of Barrow (= Quorn Park) occupied the whole of Buddon Wood, part of the site of Swithland Reservoir and much of the land in the lower right hand quarter of the photograph. (see fig. 5). It is the earliest documented creation of a deer park in the two counties.

The Creation of Breedon Park 1226

Agreement. Between Robert de Tateshal, plaintif, and Simon de Roppele, defendant of common of pasture in Tunge, namely in all the woods called 'les Cludes' and 'les Hirstes', whence the said Robert complained that Simon unjustly demanded common in the land of the said Robert in Tunge, Robert having no common in the land of the said Simon in Wurthinton, nor did Simon do service to him whereby he ought to have common. Whence a plea was summoned between them in the same court, that is to say that Simon granted for him and his heirs, as far as possible, to the said Robert, that the aforesaid woods of Cludes and Hirste shall remain park forever ,so enclosed with a fence as on the day on which this agreement was made. And for this Robert granted for him and his heirs, that the said Simon and his heirs may have twenty pigs yearly in the said park free of pannage, and likewise one buck in the time of grease (3rd May to 14t. September) and one doe in the time of hunting (11th November to 12th February) and further Robert granted for him and his heirs shall have a gate in the foreign wood of Tunge, outside the said park, for closing his —— [illegible] of Wurthinton as often as necessary, by the view of the foresters of Robert and his heirs, if he wished to come into the said wood. And if he is unwilling to come, nevertheless Simon and his heirs shall have the said closing reasonably. And if by chance at any time the said park be enclosed, the said Simon and his heirs and all the men of Wurthington, free as well as villeins, may have their common in the said park for all their cattle. And it will be lawful for Simon for all his life, as often as he may come to Wurthinton, to chase with dogs and bows and arrows, hares foxes and other beasts found in the warren of the said Robert and his heirs, of Tunge if they have a warren there.

As we have seen, most parks contained woodland as shelter for the deer along with pasture for grazing and a water supply. A park's economy was expected to make at least some contribution to its running costs, particularly the upkeep of the pale and the provision of food for the deer in winter. To this end, many were divided internally into compartments, sometimes each with a separate "park" name, occasionally giving rise to the mistaken belief by historians that there was more than one park in a given locality. Such sub-division allowed the growing of trees, the grazing of domestic stock, the digging of stone and turf and the operation of rabbit warrens and fishponds. The management of these various assets was under the control of a parker who usually lived in a modest lodge, often moated, within the park. It was also his duty to supervise the repair of the fences and to combat poaching.

The Distribution of Parks

Upwards of 1900 different hunting parks are known to have existed in England and Wales in medieval times.[2] Of these, at least fifty-five were in Leicestershire and eleven in Rutland. Several factors can be seen to account for their distribution in the two counties, the single most important of which was the presence of woodland. In the late 12th century local woodland was in short supply and unevenly distributed. Most can be traced to the entries in Domesday Book a century earlier. The incorporation of this woodland into deer parks proved to be the main factor in its survival to early modern times and even to the present.[3] Woodland was most often found where the topography was difficult for agriculture

4. *The map above, and the list opposite, show the locations of medieval parks for which reliable documentary evidence is known. The earliest source and owner for each are listed in appendix I.*

In addition to the parks shown here, there are at least three 'probable' parks, the case for which is strong but inconclusive. At both Garendon and Brooke, where there were religious houses in the middle ages, it is very likely that each community had its own hunting park, yet there is no reliable record for either. Similarly at Wymondham, there is circumstantial field name evidence, but no documentary record.

Finally, there are a further dozen or so localities where the evidence of a park ranges from 'promising' to 'mildly interesting'.

Medieval Parks in Leicestershire

1	Ashby-de-la-Zouch (= Great Park)	18	Coleorton	36	Lubbesthorpe
2	Bagworth	19	Croxton Kerrial	37	Lutterworth
3	Barn (= Barrons = Desford)	20	(Old) Dalby	38a	Market Bosworth: Old Park
4	Barrow (= Quorn)	21	Earl Shilton (= Tooley Park)	38b	Market Bosworth: Southwood Park
5	Barwell	22	Evington	39	Nailstone
6	Beaumanor	23	Foston	40	Nevill Holt
7	Beaumont Leys	24	Grace Dieu	41	Newbold Verdon
8	Belton	25	Great Easton	42	Normanton Turville (= Brokensale)
9	Belvoir	26	Groby	43	Norton-juxta-Twycross
10	Bradgate	27	Hinckley (= Sceydley Park)	44	Noseley
11	Breedon-on-the-Hill	28	Kirby Muxloe	45	Owston
12	Burbage	29	Knipton	46	Ratby
13	Burleigh	30	Langley	47	Rothley
14	Burton Lazars	31	Launde	48	Shepshed (= Oakley Park)
15	Cadeby	32	Leicester Abbey	49	Staunton Harold
16	Castle Donington	33	Leicester Frith (= Birdsnest Park)	50	Stockerston
17	Cold Overton	34	Loddington	51	Twyford
		35	Loughborough	52	Whitwick (= Bardon Park)

Medieval Parks in Rutland

1	Barnsdale	6	Hambledon	11	Ridlington
2	Burley-on-the-Hill	7	Lyddington	12	Stretton
3	Essendine	8	Market Overton	13	Whissendine
4	Exton	9	Oakham, Flitteris Park		
5	Greetham	10	Oakham, Little Park		

and where, at the same time, it enhanced the features of the park. It is hardly surprising that Charnwood Forest, with its shallow, stony and infertile soils, became ringed with a series of ten parks. The two other areas with large concentrations of parks were the rolling uplands of south-west Leicestershire and the border with Derbyshire. The creation of the parks within the Royal Forests of Leicester and Leighfield or around their margins was particularly closely connected with Domesday woodland. From an early date, Leicester Forest was under the control of the Earls of Leicester, later of Lancaster and later still Dukes of Lancaster. The creation of the parks from what was in effect their private hunting forest was part of a carefully controlled retreat from areas of declining woodland. When the second Duke ascended the throne in 1399, as King Henry IV, his lands became appended to those other estates of the Crown. By the time the Royal Forest of Leicester was finally disafforested and the land sold off in the 17th century most of the parks were in effect also in private hands.[4] A similar if less easily traced situation surrounded the foundation of the parks of Leighfield Forest, which had been even less favoured as a hunting area by medieval monarchs.

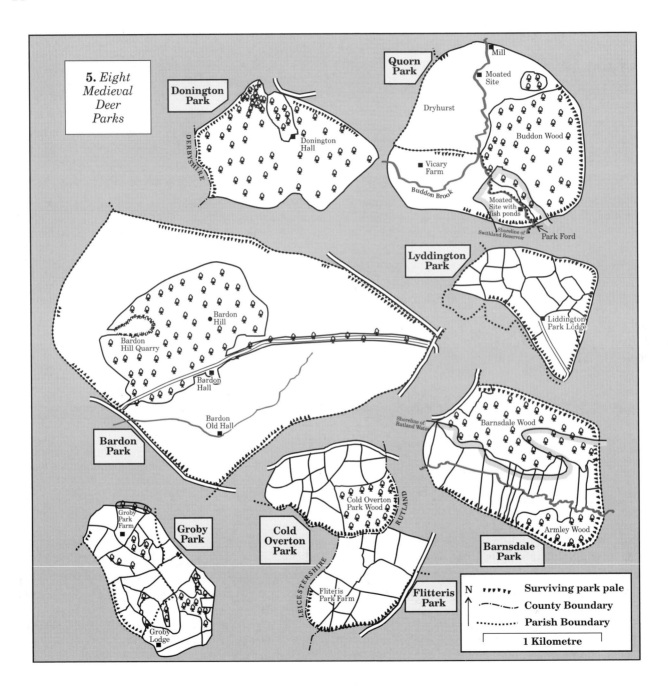

5. *Eight Medieval Deer Parks*

Donington Park

Quorn Park

Mill

Moated Site

Dryhurst

Donington Hall

DERBYSHIRE

Buddon Wood

Vicary Farm

Buddon Brook

Moated Site with fish ponds

Shoreline of Swithland Reservoir

Park Ford

Lyddington Park

Liddington Park Lodge

Bardon Hill

Bardon Hill Quarry

Bardon Hall

Bardon Old Hall

Shoreline of Rutland Water

Barnsdale Wood

Bardon Park

RUTLAND

Armley Wood

Cold Overton Park Wood

Barnsdale Park

Groby Park Farm

Groby Park

Cold Overton Park

LEICESTERSHIRE

Fliteris Park Farm

Flitteris Park

Groby Lodge

N

▾▾▾▾▾	Surviving park pale	
–··–··–	County Boundary	
·········	Parish Boundary	
	1 Kilometre	

6. *A view of Bardon Hill as seen from the south-east in 1976, before the summit was largely quarried away. The enormous medieval park of Whitwick occupied the hill top and most of the lower slopes.*

The size of Parks

The extent of a park was frequently as much a reflection of the owner's desire for status as it was on the suitability and availability for emparkment of the land he owned. Many parks started life as small enclosures and later expanded. One such was *Bardon Park*, also known as The park of *Whitwick* (see p.14) which at first was centred on a small area around the moated site of the Old Hall. Later, and in one move, it was expanded by its owner, the Earl of Buchan, to include most of the area of Bardon Hill, a total of 1260 acres. Even by national standards, this was a large park and its size was, as far as we know, not exceeded elsewhere in Leicestershire or Rutland. Another large park was that at *Beaumont Leys* which reached about 900 acres. These two compare with the 100 to 150 acres of the typical local manorial park. Smallest of all were such parks as those at *Loddington* and *Lubbesthorpe*, each of which probably did not exceed about 20 acres.

Ownership of the Parks

The ownership of the hunting parks accurately reflected the social structure of the higher levels of medieval society in general and that in our two counties in particular. The Crown held the greatest number of parks, many of which were leased out to royal favourites. *Donington Park*, in particular, had an unfortunate history in that four of its holders were executed for rebellion in the space of 100 years.[5] The Duchy of Lancaster parks in Leicestershire were part of a network which included the 11 parks of Needwood Forest in Staffordshire. The richest nobles were represented by the Earl of Huntingdon at *Exton* and *Whissendine*, the Earl of Warwick at *Greetham* and the Earl of Winchester at *Bradgate*. Successive Earls of Cornwall held Flitteris as one of a series of parks which at one time extended to 22 separate hunting areas in 11 different counties.[6]

Many of the senior clerics of the Middle Ages rose to become the social equals of their temporal brothers and enjoyed with them the advantages of high office, including holding parks. The Bishop of Lincoln, for example, held *Lyddington* as part of the benefits of his vast diocese whilst the Bishops of Durham had *Bagworth* and *Ratby* parks as two of a series of 21 parks extending over six counties.[7] At a

7. *Above: Launde seen from the west. The Abbey was situated between the West (=Big) Wood in the foreground and Park Wood, which was the site of the Abbot's Park in the middle ages.*

8. *Below: The original post-monastic house was built on the site of the Abbey and was enlarged in the 17th century. The remains of the gardens which were laid out can be found as grassy banks and ditches occupying the area between the present front door and the road which runs through the Park.*

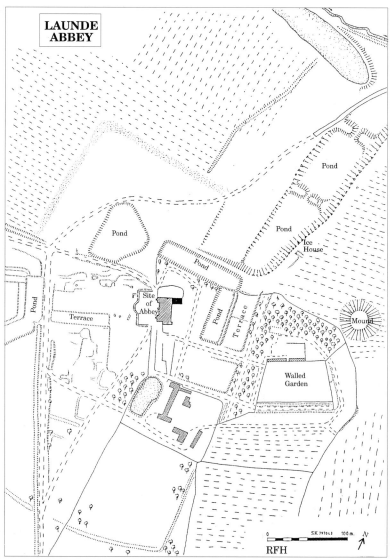

9. *The map above shows details of the monastic landscape and the changes brought about since the 1540s by successive generations of owners. Note the fishponds and the pattern of ridge and furrow created by the monks.*

more local level, several of the religious houses created parks. The wealthiest of these by far was that of the Abbey of Leicester, whose estate eventually became the second largest holding of any Augustinian House in the country. The abbot's park on the then northern edge of Leicester adjoined the abbey precincts to the north-west and came to extend over much of the land of the present Blackbird Road area. The other major but less wealthy houses in the county – *Launde* (shown opposite), *Croxton* (see p.18), *Owston*, and *Dalby* also had parks on their demesne land. Even the prioresses of *Grace Dieu* and *Langley* had small parks adjacent to their respective priory sites. In addition, the Hospitals of Lutterworth and Burton Lazars had small fenced enclosures for deer. Finally, a group of newly enriched knightly families made their marks on the local landscape. These included the Tatershals of *Breedon*, who created a second park at *Cold Overton*, and the Shirleys of *Staunton Harold*.

Although some survived well into the 16th century, and even to the present, many of the hunting parks of the two counties were very short lived affairs. The location for the park of Grace Dieu at

Belton was a poor choice since it occupied fertile land on a south facing slope which was well drained and easy to cultivate. Consequently, by the early 14th century it had been relocated to a site adjacent to the priory on Charnwood Forest. *Ratby* park was created in the very early thirteenth century and was later expanded by Anthony Bek, Bishop of Durham (d. 1310). The site provided a disadvantageous line for the pale and the park was clearly difficult and expensive to maintain. *Burbage* park is known from a single reference in 1289 and *Stretton* from a single one in 1219. This absence of documentary evidence may not necessarily indicate that these parks were short-lived, but it seems likely. Similarly, in east Leicestershire, *Great Easton* park is first heard of in the 1220s but not again after 1236. The end of many parks in the following century as a result of the arrival of the Black Death in 1348, and subsequent plagues, can be detected in the fall of rental values.

10. *Abbey Park, Leicester (from the west). The site of the monastery of St. Mary-in-the-Meadows is located adjacent to the prominent oval of trees in the middle of the picture. During the Middle Ages the abbot's deer park extended over much of the lower middle foreground of the view.*

11. *Croxton Park between Croxton Kerrial and Waltham-on-the-Wolds, from the southwest. The Abbey stood on land to the upper right of the two largest pools (centre of picture) where earthworks can be clearly seen. The early medieval park occupied much of the land to the top left of the abbey site, and between the two broad belts of woodland.*

At *Owston* the park was valued only as a "summer pasture" and the park of *Stockerston* disappears from the records by 1367.

The legacy of the hunting parks

Five and more centuries after most of them were abandoned, signs of their former presence are widespread on the local landscape. In many places sections of the bank and ditch of the pale may be found, often following an ancient parish boundary. At Bardon, for example, a quarter of a mile of bank and ditch, redundant for retaining deer since very early in the 14th century, survives in a spinney alongside the road from Copt Oak to Abbots Oak. At *Lyddington*, a similar but even more remarkable bank and ditch marks the eastern boundary of the Bishop of Lincoln's park. At other places such as *Breedon* and *Bagworth*, only small fragments survive in hedge lines or in woodland.

Parks in the later Middle Ages

The effects of the Black Death and subsequent plagues undoubtedly resulted in the abandonment of many hunting parks. However, by the latter part of the fifteenth century, growing prosperity and changing social and economic conditions promoted the establishment of entirely new parks. Most of these later creations bore more resemblance to the amenity parks of Tudor and Stuart times than they did to their predecessors. They were less numerous but often larger in size. They usually lacked the bank and ditch of the medieval pale and were often sited on otherwise fertile arable land which was converted to pasture.

About ten such parks are known for Leicestershire and Rutland. Outstanding among their creators was William Hastings, one of the leading nobles at the court of Edward IV. In 1474, he was granted licence to empark 3000 acres at *Ashby* and 2000 acres at each of his other manors of *Kirby Muxloe* and *Bagworth*.[8] Whether or not he was able to carry out his plans at the last two places is unclear but he certainly created three parks at Ashby. Two of these were the Little Park which adjoined his castle garden and Prestop Park to the north-west of the town. His Great Park was "ten miles in compace" and was created from the earlier hunting park of about 60 acres.[9] It was centred on the site of the present Eastern and Western Old Parks Farms. All three parks contained deer until well into Elizabeth's reign and were finally abandoned in the 17th century.

At *Nevill Holt,* in 1448, Sir Thomas Palmer emparked, under licence from the Crown, his demesne land to the south of his hall.[10] In so doing he re-routed the course of the road from Nevill Holt to Drayton;

13. *Bardon Park. A surviving section of the pale which effectively became redundant in the early four-teenth century. It lies in a spinney alongside the road from Copt Oak to Abbots Oak.*

but he was unable or unwilling to realign the parish boundary with Great Easton so the eastern edge of the park shows an irregular or "jagged" outline characteristic of some of these later creations.

Medieval Gardens

The garden plots of the late Saxon period were small and were most often used to supply the basic culinary and medicinal needs of a household rather than for pleasure and recreation. Gardening was based on possibly fewer than 100 different plant species, the great majority of which were herbs, vegetables and vines.[11] However, monks from continental religious houses and crusaders returning from southern Europe meant new ideas, skills and plant species came to English gardens. Yet it was only the Crown and the higher nobles who were able to take advantage of these innovations. With them lay the development of the garden form which we now regard as typical of the Middle Ages.

12. *The last remnant of the pale of Bagworth Park is in a hedgeline, now part of the modern field pattern.*

Much of what we know of their gardens comes less from written records than from illustrations in books and manuscripts, especially those from France. Garden plots were small and were square or rectangular in outline. Each was enclosed by a low wall or a hedge of carefully pruned trees or bushes. Typically there was a trellis up which climbing plants such as roses or honeysuckle were trained. Separated thus from their surroundings, they were havens of peace and privacy where their noble owners might entertain, give court or conduct business and private conversations.

The interiors of these early gardens were composed of formal beds, again square or rectangular, the soil of which was sometimes raised above the grassy or gravel paths which led between and around them.[12] Flowers and sweet smelling herbs were set out in formal lines, blocks and patterns within the beds. In some places small patches of grass were also laid out. These were known at the time as lawns; but they also contained flowering plants other than grasses and today we would more readily recognise them as meadows. At points around their perimeters benches of wood or stone were placed. They were topped with turf which was planted with flowers which gave off a sweet scent when crushed by the sitter. In other places small trees including fruit trees were trained and pruned to desired shapes.

Our knowledge of gardens improves considerably from the beginning of the 13th century which, it will be recalled, was the high period of park creation in England. Leaving aside the small plots of peasant holdings, we can recognise some of the elements of the gardens of the well-to-do. Once again, the location and layout of the garden reflected the wealth, rank and aspirations of the owner. Gardens were often multi-purpose in nature and would be seen as part of a complex of buildings and spaces within the curtilage of the lord's dwelling.

The terms used at the time to describe gardens are sometimes difficult to define since they were often inter-changeable and seem to us to have been employed with a lack of precision. The typical garden resembled its predecessor with its formal beds of flowers and herbs with gravel paths and turf benches. Oddly enough, it was sometimes referred to as the 'yard', a term for a rear garden which has survived to the present in the Midlands and the north of England. This flower garden might contain a central statue or sun-dial as a focal point. The arbour, or herber, was an area where a fence in the form of a curve, an arch or a tunnel, covered with honeysuckle, allowed particular privacy from the eyes of the persons in the adjoining buildings.[13] The poet Chaucer had one such garden in which he found refuge from the troubles of the world:

> Hoom to min hous ful swiftly I me spedde
> To goon to reste, and early for to ryse,
> To seen this flour to sprede, as I devyse.
> And a litel herber that I have,
> That benched was on turves fresshe y-grave
> I bad men sholde me my couche make. . . .

Closely associated with the garden, and even integrated with it, was the pomarium or orchard. This was primarily given over to the production of fruit but the ground beneath the trees could also be used for cultivating vegetables. More often it was laid down to grass, the meadow or "scented mead", to be cut or grazed or otherwise managed to a profit. Adjoining the garden was the dovehouse, the inhabitants of which provided a visual delight, soothing background sounds and, not least, a supply of fresh meat in the winter.

The Later Medieval Garden

During the second half of the 15th century new ideas and fashions in garden design and content reached Britain from Burgundy and the Low Countries. The regular straight lines of boundary hedges and fences remained, as did the formal internal layout, but the nature of the cultivation and the species concerned were changing. The art of topiary, the trimming of bushes and small trees to desired shapes, first makes its appearance at this time. Also developed from religious sources was the maze or labyrinth, the origins of which were based on ideas of mystery and penance. Mazes of various kinds are, of course, well known today but in the Middle Ages they were always trimmed below knee height and they could also be of turf, as in the one of unknown date at *Wing* in Rutland today. Other additions to gardens were the heraldic beasts. These were large, made of wood and painted in bright colours. They were set at intervals among the beds, the better to proclaim the status of the noble owner and the pedigree of his family.[14]

As the Middle Ages drew to a close and the threat of destruction from warfare diminished, gardening flourished over a wider landscape. Gardens increased in number and became larger, more complex and varied in form. Features such as the knot garden and the prospect mound of later Tudor times made their first appearance. Gardens were also developed on moated sites which were largely being abandoned as dwelling places at this time.

The medieval gardens of Leicestershire and Rutland fall into four broad categories according to the buildings to which they were attached: castles, grand houses, monastic sites and manor houses. To these may be added the gardens of the houses of the people of the town of Leicester.

Castle Gardens

There are few records of gardens in the motte and bailey castles which were thrown up in the early years after the Norman Conquest. Many of the substantial stone structures which replaced them certainly had gardens, some of which were outside the castle walls and ditches. At Windsor, a range of such gardens was developed for different purposes. Unfortunately, with the exception of that at Leicester, there were no other castles of any real size and importance in the two counties. In view of the shortage of written records, any assessment must be made on archaeological discoveries, our knowledge of castles in other areas and on the records of later centuries.

Leicester Castle (figure 14, below) was founded shortly after 1066 as a motte and bailey. For two centuries it was the fortified residence of the Earls of Leicester and later Lancaster. After it had passed

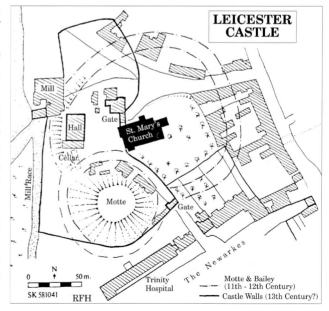

to the crown in 1399 it lost much of its importance. A stone outer baily was erected in the later Middle Ages to include the area known as the Newark. Within the castle enclosure was an "old garden", the herbage of which in 1322 was worth 4s 4d yearly.[15] There is also mention of "the lord's herber" which seems to have been a separate private area. A second garden, the "new garden", also existed at the time. It was at a place outside the wall where a certain John Coventry also held a plot.[16] In the same year six perches of hedge were made around the new garden and eleven and a half perches were erected around it and the grange, below the castle wall and opposite the mill. The sale of the herbage there, where a man cultivated the vines for the vintner, was worth 1s 6d a year.[17] The site of this "new garden" appears to have been in that open area known today as Castle Gardens and that of the "old garden" in the area to the north of the Castle Yard in the area of the present Castle Street.

The early castle at *Oakham* consisted of a timber hall which stood upon a motte within a bailey. Part of this motte is still distinguishable in the south-east corner. The curtain wall was erected in the 13th century and was rebuilt and repaired at different times.[18] In 1340 the walls enclosed approximately two acres of land within which was a garden valued at 8s yearly. Outside the walls there was a preserve with a dike of yearly value 3s 4d. which was also associated with a moat and fishponds.[19] Fifty years later the fruit and herbage of the garden within the

castle were worth 12d and those outside 10s.[20] The garden, moat and fishponds can be identified with the area known today as Cutts Close which forms a large court or outer baily to the north.

The castle at *Ashby-de-la-Zouch*, now a towering ruin, was constructed in the late fifteenth century by the Hastings family on the site of an earlier manor house. To the south of the southern courtyard is an area known as "The Wilderness" where the earthworks of an early garden are some of the most impressive in the county. These may be

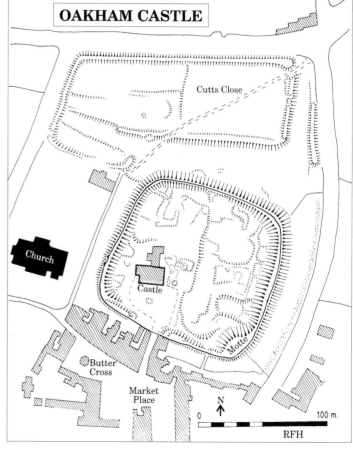

OAKHAM CASTLE

Cutts Close

Church

Castle

Motte

Butter Cross

Market Place

N

0   100 m.

RFH

---

15. *Oakham Castle. The castle originated in 1180 as a motte and bailey structure. Part of the motte (mound) can be seen in the right hand corner of the enclosure. The gardens and other appurtenances of the castle are seen in the earthworks at the top of the plan in an area now known as Cutts Close.*

16. *Right and*
17. *Below right:*
Ashby Castle,
now in ruins,
was built in the
15th century.
The formal
gardens were
laid out to the
south but were
probably not con-
temporary with
the building of
the castle

18. *Below left:*
The view from
the top of the
Hastings Tower.
The earthworks
shown are those
on the eastern
half of the site.

contemporary with the building of the Castle but are more likely to date from the following century. There are also two garden towers which were probably part of the same garden plan.

Of the remaining castles for which records survive that at *Belvoir* had an orchard worth 53s 4d yearly in 1440.[21] At *Donington*, in the early 14th century, Henry de Lacy held two gardens "within and without the castle" which produced "herbage" worth 2s yearly.[22] Although twenty years later the buildings were ruinous, the garden outside the castle had lost none of its value. Shortly after the Black Death had visited the town John, Earl of Kent, held "a certain orchard below the castle" which had "pasture" worth 2s yearly.[23]

Grand Houses

It has until recently been thought that the Grey's mansion at Bradgate, a truly magnificent house of its time, was begun about the year 1490 and completed a decade or so later. Recent work, however, suggests the building was erected somewhat later (see p. 45). This leaves a single example of a major new house at the end of the Middle Ages – *Kirby Muxloe Castle* near Leicester. This was begun in 1480 by William Lord Hastings whose rise to wealth and prominence we have already noted. The modest house and garden of his ancestors was replaced by a large country house, constructed in brick and moated around. There was to be a great gatehouse and towers at four corners to give the impression of a castle. Although work on the project ceased abruptly after Hastings' execution in 1483, details of the site and the surviving building accounts provide some oblique references to the proposed gardens. These were to be fenced around with oak palings. John Peyntour, one of the gardeners who were all classed as labourers, was instructed to "gather" crab trees "for grafts to be done therefrom". The site of the orchard was to be outside the moat as "thorns for hedges" were needed to separate it from the adjacent park.[24]

Monastic Gardens

The emphasis in monastic gardens was on the production of herbs for medicinal purposes and the growing of flowers for decoration and worship. Communal relaxation in a garden setting was usually restricted to the area of the cloisters and in some establishments the prior or abbot had a private garden of his own.

Apart from Leicester Abbey, there were no large local religious houses as judged by national standards. At its surrender to the Crown in 1538, Leicester Abbey had both a garden and a park. A contemporary description of the site makes no direct mention of the former but refers to a "fayr orchard" to the south of the main abbey buildings and also to a cloister, which probably contained a garden.[25] The area to the south-east of the buildings was described in 1571 as three large closes "containing the traces of fishponds, terraces and walks".[26] In addition, the substantial wall we see today around the western edge of the site, erected by Abbot Penny, contained seats.

Most of Leicestershire's religious houses were small on account of their late foundations, and poor because their estates were small and composed of scattered holdings. The tiny house of Bradley near Great Easton surrendered at the Dissolution, "an orchard and garden hedged with quick with a little pond and well set with young fruit trees". The area covered one rood and ten poles and the total produce was worth 6s 8d a year or about 3% of the income of the demesne.[27] At Grace Dieu the garden was about two acres in extent and enclosed by a wall. It had been designed by the nuns to resemble their vision of the Garden of Gethsemane.[28]

Glover del. 1790.

19. *Above: The Moat House at Appleby Magna. When Nichols published this view in 1811 the house was regarded as something of a curiosity. The large building to the right is the gatehouse. The two buidlings are the surviving remnants of a larger group of buildings.*

20. *Left: Plan of the Moat House site. East of the church a small stone-based dovecote (1) stands on a slight promontory. The surrounding hollowed out area (2) might have been dammed to form a pond. By the church wall is a terrace (3) which formerly had farm buildings on it. The structures within the moat itself comprise a stone gatehouse (4) of 15th. century date, and a timber frame house (5) not later than the 16th. century. To the south is a small rectangular pond. (6) The area of low rectangular earthworks (7) may indicate the site of a garden, divided into four parts in the traditional pattern. Beyond this is a hollow way (8), apparently an old back lane, and a small paddock (9) called the 'bull ring' containing some traces of possible building foundations.*

Manor Houses

At the lowest end of the social scale of garden makers were the prosperous knightly families and wealthy gentlemen with incomes of up to about one hundred pounds per year. These local leaders lived in substantial manor houses, few of which have survived to the present without major modification. A typical dwelling such as that at Appleby Magna had a moat, both as a status symbol and as a means of defence. In some cases the moat may simply have been constructed as a garden feature.

Our knowledge of the layout and extent of the gardens, buildings and closes of these modest manorial sites is far from perfect. The manor house

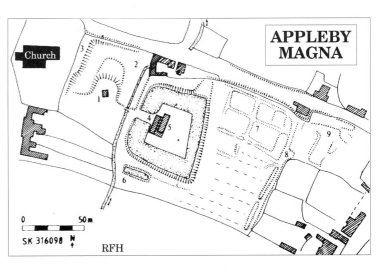

APPLEBY MAGNA

Church

SK 316098   N

RFH

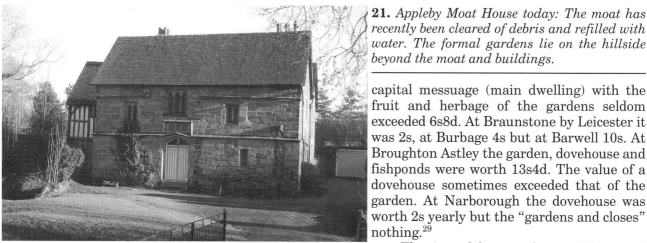

21. *Appleby Moat House today: The moat has recently been cleared of debris and refilled with water. The formal gardens lie on the hillside beyond the moat and buildings.*

capital messuage (main dwelling) with the fruit and herbage of the gardens seldom exceeded 6s8d. At Braunstone by Leicester it was 2s, at Burbage 4s but at Barwell 10s. At Broughton Astley the garden, dovehouse and fishponds were worth 13s4d. The value of a dovehouse sometimes exceeded that of the garden. At Narborough the dovehouse was worth 2s yearly but the "gardens and closes" nothing.[29]

at Donington-le-Heath, dating from the year 1280, is Leicestershire's oldest house but no documentary records of its early years survive. However, the home of the Ferrers at Groby was probably typical although only tiny fragments of the early fabric survive.

Some records of gardens emphasise the production of fruit and vegetables. In the late 13th and early 14th centuries the annual values of the

The sizes of these gardens and the actual flowers and vegetables they contained are even more difficult to determine. Most gardens seldom exceeded two or three acres, although Sir Robert Swillinton's garden at Kirby Bellars extended over about ten acres. In contrast, the second of two gardens at Burton Overy was "a small plot 25 feet long". There were vineyards at Newbold Verdon[30] and Wymondham,[31] and at Bottesford a garden had

22. *Right: Groby Old Hall c. 1811 (seen from the NW – not NE as stated in Nichols IV, pt 2,).*
The 14th century 'Towerhill' gardens occupied the area to the left of the house. The text of the IPM describes various buildings ranged around a 'cloister'. This complex most likely extended from the main hall towards the figure in the foreground.
23. *Opposite: The photograph is taken from the towerhill mound, across the the 14th C. gardens, to the much altered present day house.*

Groby Old Hall and Gardens in the 14th Century

In the site of the manor [there is] one cellar under the vault next the cloister and a chamber above the cellar aforesaid and a lower chamber between the said cellar and the wall of the manor towards the west and south sides next the chapel as far as the chamber above the hall which is called Sir Henry Ferrers' Chamber; and the chapel of the manor next the cloister, and one inner chamber under the lord's chief chamber towards the west side and the whole plot from the kitchen chamber between the site of the manor and the wall of the same manor towards the south and west sides. And of a garden which is called 'le Tourhull' [Towerhill] the third part towards the west, as it appears by the bounds there made by a certain ancient ditch there which is called 'la Glade'; and one grave [grove] which is called 'le Heyburn' [Hay barn]; and the longhouse which is called 'Vercar' and one entire house next the small gates, which is called 'le Bailiffes House', and one entire dovecote next the house aforesaid; and of a certain garden, viz. ,from the ditch which is called 'le Napeler' ditch the third part towards the east, with free exit and ingress to the great gates.

This important Inquisition Post Mortem contains the earliest known reference to a garden in Leicestershire. Given here is an extract describing that part of the manor of Groby which was assigned in 1343 to Isabella, wife of the late Henry Ferrers (lord of Groby), as her dower. The description is of the then Groby Hall and its associated buildings and gardens. Seen together with two similar documents of 1371 and 1388,later references and an 18th century map, one can deduce something of the layout of this important manor house, typical of the 14th century and very different from the one we see today.

The house itself consisted of a principal chamber, the Hall, with smaller rooms above and to the sides. These included a withdrawing chamber and the lord's own chamber. Below ground there were cellars, at least one of which was a wine cellar. Other essential buildings which accompanied the dwelling included the chapel opposite the hall, the kitchen, and the new and old pantries. They were ranged around a square or rectangular cloister which lay to the west of the Hall. Other buildings of this complex were the bailiff's house, the gatehouse and the chapel yard. Further to the west, but in the immediate vicinity, were the buildings of an agricultural nature which served the needs of the complex: the forgehouse the barnyard, the byre, the stable, the sheepcote and the dovehouse.

There were also two gardens. The first appears to have occupied a position to the south of the principal buildings. The second, the Towerhill Garden, lay to the north and west. The Towerhill in question was the remains of the motte of the early motte and bailey castle which had been erected here in the 11th. century and which was destroyed in the following one. In a modified form it remains to this date, between the Hall and the Groby Bypass. The entire site; Hall, associated buildings and gardens lay within the surviving 11th century bailey ditch. The area of land which this enclosed was large even by national standards. It is likely that Towerhill continued to be used as a garden with little modification until the 16th century when Thomas Grey, Marquis of Dorset, filled it in when he relandscaped the area. Allowing for further redevelopment of the site over the centuries, it seems likely from field inspection that the 14th century Towerhill Garden lay immediately adjacent to the Hall it served and that sections of the 11th century ditch were employed as garden features and planted accordingly.

100 apple trees worth 2s each,40 pear trees worth 3s4d each and 60 plum trees worth 12d each.[32]

The Town of Leicester

Leicester was the only sizeable town in either county in the Middle Ages and an idea of its nature and layout can be gained from Speed's map of 1611 or that of Roberts of 1741 (shown opposite). Both show a town which changed only slowly between the Conquest and the Industrial Revolution of the late 18th and early 19th centuries. We have seen that the town rose to prominence in the 13th and 14th centuries. By the middle of the latter the population had reached about 6,000, of which a third were carried off by a number of outbreaks of the Black Death, following its first appearance in 1348. At the beginning of Elizabeth's reign (1558-1603) there were about 600 households of which a little over half, the wealthier section of the population, lived within the city walls. The remainder were found in the suburbs which had grown up outside the North, South and East Gates. It was not until the end of the 17th century that the total population attained its pre-plague numbers.[33]

The area of the Roman City within the walls occupied something over 100 acres and the unequal distribution of the inhabitants was marked. The greatest concentration was along the streets of the business and commercial area to the south. Here were the butchers, shoemakers, tailors, mercers, weavers and a large number of other traders whose combined activities could hardly be said to have imparted an industrial character to the town.

The details of the buildings as shown on Roberts' map (see page 26) suggests a level of crowding that was not present in the Middle Ages.[34] There was no separation of home from business and many of the tradesmen kept domestic stock on their plots or had farming interests beyond the walls in the town's great open fields. In many places the burgage plots, shown in stylized form on Roberts' map, contained well separated barns, gardens and stables, in addition to the places of work. Some large houses were accompanied by large gardens with orchards. It was a town which, even in the most populous parts, reflected the dual basis of agriculture and industry on which the livelihood of most people depended.

Lists of freemen and taxation records of the 13th century note the activities of a few professional gardeners, although most men worked their own plots on a family basis. In 1352 William Black signed over to his brother Ralph all his rights to "an orchard in the city and four plots in the suburbs". A law case in 1394 settled a dispute over two tenements which were identified by the five gardens of four different owners which abutted them. One particular garden in Soapers Lane was divided among the members of one family to give each of them a garden.

The High Cross, the focal centre of the town and the most prosperous area, was surrounded by gardens. The nearby church of St. Martin was destroyed in 1173 and the streets became green lanes. The sites of the houses were converted into orchards and remained as such until eventual redevelopment in the later Middle Ages.

Some gardens were very large, especially in the north. Most of the records for St. Michael's parish concerned orchards, gardens, dovecotes and plots of ground rather than buildings. One garden here was bounded by 88 ashes and two aspen trees. Gardens and crofts extended along Parchment Lane and those belonging to the wealthy citizens were attached to St. John's Hospital or the Corpus Christi Guild in Soapers Lane.

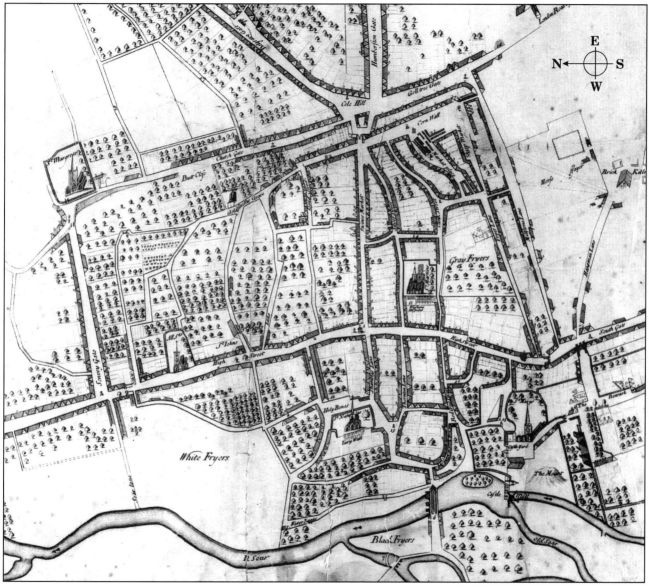

24. *Detail from Roberts' map of Leicester, dated 1741. Note how the numerous gardens and few buildings in the north of the town give it an open nature which contrasts with the crowded areas in the south, where the majority of the population lived.*

CHAPTER TWO
Tudor and Stuart Parks and Gardens

The development of the parks and gardens during the period 1500-1660 was influenced by many diverse factors: the arrival of peace and stability after the wars of the 15th century, the Dissolution of the Monasteries and the flooding of the property market with land and buildings, the rising rural prosperity enjoyed by certain groups of the population and the inability of the Stuart monarchs to manage their finances. Finally, there was the Civil War which brought devastation to many properties and financial ruin to their owners. This century and a half saw the house and garden move to the park but remain separate from it. Not until the 18th century did park, house and garden become part and parcel of the same grand design.

PARKS

The most important development in the 16th century was the abandonment of the hunting park, a place primarily for sport, distant from the owner's dwelling, heavily fenced and closely guarded, and its replacement by the "amenity" park. Here the lord built his principal residence, or at least a lodge, with its attendant gardens. Both park and gardens were built separately but with the common aim of enhancing the dwelling. Many 16th century parks were on the site of earlier enclosures but were larger than their predecessors had been. Most had a perimeter pale but this usually lacked the earlier bank and ditch, since hunting was of secondary importance. A simple but stout fence now controlled the movement of domestic stock and contained the deer with which they shared the grazing.

Changing social and economic factors influenced the development of the parks. In the first place the end of feudalism brought a decline in the power of the nobility which it maintained. There was a rise in the fortunes of the gentleman and yeoman classes which was associated with the rising rural prosperity and the expansion of the population which accompanied it. The social structure of Elizabethan England was arranged on strictly hierarchical grounds, but movement between the ranks was relatively easy. A man with new wealth could buy out a family in decline. The possession of a park was as much a demonstration of social rank as was a coat of arms.

The first half of the 16th century saw much park creation, but in later years many parks were abandoned as the rising population created a demand for more arable land. Depopulation of rural areas was illegal but it still took place. Parks were divided into individual farms and let out on long leases. The parks of Leicestershire and Rutland of this time have left surprisingly few records. Emparkment usually required royal approval and disparkment was supposed to be accompanied by at least a formal statement to that effect, but many parks slipped quietly out of existence. Not surprisingly, perhaps, successive generations of 16th and early 17th century map makers, who copied shamelessly from the efforts of their predecessors, sometimes had great difficulty in deciding what was and what was not a park. For the purposes of this chapter a park of those times will be considered as an area of land which contained a principal residence or lodge and with specific boundaries which were firmly fenced so as to make it a discrete unit. This parkland was composed wholly or mostly of pasture which was grazed by domestic stock and/or deer. It also contained trees set singly in a "parkland" setting or planted in more substantial spinneys or small woods.

The parks of this chapter fall into two broad categories: those which had survived from the Middle Ages and which belonged to the Crown, the nobles, the monasteries, or the gentry; and those which were in effect new creations.

The Monastic Parks

In our two counties two men were the chief beneficiaries of monastic sites and the parks which accompanied them. The first was Thomas Cromwell, the man who engineered the Dissolution on a national scale and the second was Thomas Manners, Earl of Rutland. To the former passed the parks of *Launde, Loddington* and *Lyddington*, although Cromwell and his descendants were to enjoy them for only a short time. Manners acquired *Garendon, Belvoir,* and *Croxton.* He attempted to extend the boundaries of his Garendon property and develop the site which the monks had held. Deer were introduced and may well have maintained an unbroken presence until the entire herd was shot during World War Two.

The Royal Parks

The surviving royal parks were those of the Duchy of Lancaster which had been part of the Royal Forest of Leicester together with those which had been associated with the Royal Forest of Leighfield. Both Forests were deafforested and the land sold off in the 1630s after they had become more valuable to the crown for grazing sheep than hunting deer. *Barrons Park* containing about 250 acres, was well wooded and in the early sixteenth century contained pasture enough for a total of 250 bullocks and horses in addition to that reserved for the deer.[1]

Tooley Park was larger at about 450 acres and maintained a long history of woodland cover and grazing. In 1608 it contained 3,500 trees worth almost 1,000 pounds.[2] *Beaumont Leys*, including Beaumont Wood, at more than 900 acres was the largest of the group. In 1524 visitors reported seeing at least 800 deer here and reckoned there was additional feeding for 400 sheep.[3] Two years later the park was divided into two parts.[4] There are no more mentions of deer and, as Leland noted, "Beaumont Leys sumtyme a great park by Leicester (is) now converted to pasture".

The former large *Leicester Frith Park* was reduced in size by Henry VIII and given a new lease of life in 1526 under the name of *New Park*.[5] This too was at first well stocked with deer; but the monarch quickly tired of his new venture and by 1606 its 700 acres had been fenced and drained and were worth 400 pounds a year as sheep pasture.[6]

The disposal of the site of Leicester Abbey and its park, an extensive and valuable property to the north of the town, took place at the highest level. In 1551, the park contained deer and extended over 180 acres of pasture, meadow and woodland. The initial grant was to William Parr, the King's brother-in-law.[7] It subsequently passed through the families of Hastings and Hatton and thence to the Cavendishes. The ruins of the mansion which William Cavendish built can be seen in the modern *Abbey Park*.

At an early date the Crown had lost interest in its park at *Hinckley*. By 1589 it had declined to the status of a wood[8] and passed through several keeperships before 1622, when Burton noted it had been disparked. At *Donington* (see p.14) the park was of an entirely different nature and was under Duchy of Lancaster control. At the Dissolution the keepership was granted to the Grays of Langley who built a lodge and increased the area to accommodate more sheep. In 1595 the Park was acquired by Sir George Hastings of Gopsall. It was his family who replaced the lodge with a stone hall around which were laid out ponds, gardens and avenues of trees.[9]

Three parks associated with the Forest of Leighfield survived into the 16th century. *Flitteris* Park (see p.14) contained deer in 1521 but declined soon after, to become a park in name only.[10] *Brooke* Park was held for much of the century by the Harringtons but its history as a park is unknown. The same family held *Ridlington* Park which included large quantities of woodland. By 1622 it was outside the bounds of the Royal Forest and was disparked, to be deafforested shortly afterwards.

Parks of the Nobility and Gentry

The third group of medieval survivors was in the hands of the nobility and gentry. Of the noble interest four families dominated the scene: Hastings, Grey, Cecil and, later, Villiers. The Greys, based at Groby owned *Bradgate* and *Groby* Parks and just before their downfall in 1554, those at *Burleigh*,

Loughborough and *Market Bosworth*. The Hastings subsequently regained *Burleigh* and *Loughborough*, and at *Ashby* they expanded their early enclosure to create the Great Park to the east of the town. In addition, their two other parks, *Prestop Park* and *Little Park* also contained deer until well into the 17th century.[11]

At *Lyddington* (see p.14) the park was acquired in 1551 by the Cecils, the family who built that most stately of Elizabethan houses, Burghley House, near Stamford, Lincolnshire. Lyddington remained in the family for more than 300 years, but its life as a park probably ceased at an early date since it contained nothing more than a hunting lodge.

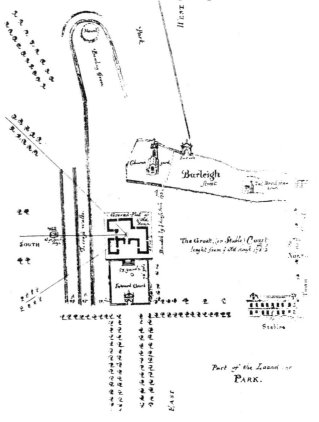

25. *Burley-on-the-Hill, 1655, showing the basic plan of the house, burnt down in the Civil War, and gardens created by George Villiers, Duke of Buckingham. Note the terraced walkways, prospect mount, bowling green and the formal avenues of trees. (From Finch, 1901) Note the confusion of the spelling 'Burleigh' on this map. With this exception 'Burleigh' refers to the park near Loughborough throughout this book.*

In early Stuart times the activities of the Villiers family made a considerable impact on the landscape of the two counties. From modest beginnings as the son of the squire of Brooksby, George Villiers (1592-1628), a royal favourite, rose rapidly up the social scale to become Duke of Buckingham in 1623. He purchased the manor of Oakham and brought about much-needed renovations to the castle. He also acquired *Garendon* park with its deer from his wife's family. Yet his greatest achievement was his purchase of *Burley-on-the-Hill* (see plan opposite). Here, he erected a splendid new mansion with gardens, expanded the park and filled it with deer. His death in 1628 broke the family's links with Oakham and Garendon but those at Burley survived even the Civil War.

New Creations

The new parks which appeared in response to changing economic trends in the agriculture of the times were usually the work of ruthless men like Sir Thomas Hazlerig of Noseley who emparked 940 acres of his demesne between the years 1504 and 1509. In so doing he depopulated the village of Noseley and laid down the former ploughland to sheep pasture. In effect cultivation ceased and he was prosecuted, only to receive a royal pardon.[12] At *Newhall* in Thurlaston, Sir William Turville received

26. *Right: Wistow from the east. Shortly after purchasing the manor in the 17th century, the Halfords emparked their demesne and built a new house, represented here by the present building (upper right) which was modernised in the 18th and 19th centuries. The ridge and furrow of the early village shows clearly.*

27. *Below: Wistow in 1636. The Hall is shown with formal gardens, parts of which appear to have been parterres. Emparkment left the church isolated from the village.*

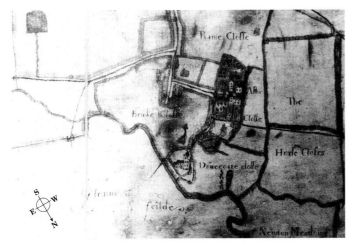

licence to create a new park. This was unusual for two reasons: firstly, it was a park shaped on medieval lines, with a pale of bank, ditch and fence; and secondly the boundary of the Royal Forest of Leicester ran through the park rather than around it.[13] His deer attracted poachers and this enclosure had certainly been disparked by 1622. At *Quenby* the long-resident Ashby family had acquired the entire manor by 1563 and moved to enclose and depopulate

28. *Stapleford Park near Melton Mowbray seen from the west. The park was created by William Sherard in 1627 and extended in stages over the next two centuries by later generations of his family. The earthworks marking the site of the former village can be seen running off the photograph on the middle left. The ridge and furrow of the former inhabitants also shows clearly on the right. The Hall is now used as an hotel.*

shortly afterwards.[14] They went on to build a great country house which dominated the area.

Early in the 17th century the Halfords of Clipston in Northamptonshire bought the manor of *Wistow* (figs. 26 and 27). Enclosure of the parish had been completed by 1632, at about which time the village was depopulated, a move which left the church surrounded by fields.[15] The Noel family similarly emparked their demesne at *Kirkby Mallory*. The manor descended through the Maynard family and the site of the park is now occupied by the well known race track.

At *Stapleford*, near Melton Mowbray, (shown opposite) William Sherard, ennobled in 1627 as Baron Leitrim, created around his hall the modest park which was later extended over the following two centuries by his descendants.

Possibly the most unusual park creation of the time was that of Sir Henry Beaumont. There had been a deer park at *Coleorton* long before the Beaumonts but it had fallen into disuse. Sir Henry, who had made a fortune from his coalmines, re-emparked in 1606, with bank, ditch and fence. This new enclosure lay to the north of his new hall but to the south of the earlier site. Much of the new

29. *The bank and ditch (to the right) of the pale of Coleorton Park. This section was part of that enclosing Spring Wood and, along with the remainder of the site, was destroyed by opencast mining in 1988. This feature is remarkable since it was constructed by Sir Henry Beaumont in 1606 but to all intents and purposes is identical in form to its medieval predecessors.*

park occupied the area from which he and his predecessors had extracted coal.[16] It is perhaps not too difficult to imagine the scene of deer grazing over the grass-covered spoil heaps and around the mouths of abandoned mine shafts.

GARDENS

The gardens of early Tudor and Stuart England experienced some marked and important changes. The achievements of this period, in which the Renaissance ideas spread throughout England, were as marked in gardening as they were in music, art, science and literature. The spread of cultural ideas to this country from Italy was accompanied by England's growing economic and political importance. Exploration beyond Europe brought not only an increase in trade and wealth but also the discovery and importation of large numbers of new plant species, many of which proved suitable for English soils and the English climate. As experiment replaced tradition in the garden and herbalism gave way to the study of botany, English gardens flourished as never before.

It was the royal court and the richer nobles who, as ever, gave a lead and set the fashions. Many families improved, adapted or added to the gardens of their ancestors. Others, such as Lord Burghley at Theobalds, in Hertfordshire, and Sir Christopher Hatton at Holdenby, in Northamptonshire, created extravagant new gardens at enormous cost. As gardening quickly became established as a worthy pursuit of gentle folk, the desire for a garden to reflect wealth and status, reached downwards through the social scale to the ranks of the country gentlemen and the wealthier yeomen.

The basic rectangular or square form of the medieval garden persisted, but the Elizabethan garden was altogether larger and differed markedly in detail. The central and defining feature was the appearance of the raised beds of the Knot Garden. A knot was created by laying out plants in geometrical patterns, with the borders and main lines composed of strips which contrasted markedly with one another. The spaces between were sometimes filled with flowers; alternatively, sand or pebbles were used. The intricacy of the design was achieved by intertwining the lines to form the "under" and "over" of a knot.

Such gardens were surrounded by clipped hedges and through them a series of paths was laid out. Between the geometrical beds and along the borders might be found fountains, grottoes, caves and specimens of the art of topiary. Raised walkways or terraces were often constructed and elevated views of the garden might also be obtained from prospect mounds. The total concept and layout of the Elizabethan garden were based on a complex of artistic, religious and political considerations. Nothing was left to chance. There was no ad hoc or piecemeal approach to design, although its actual implementation might well be carried out over a number of years.

Towards the end of the 16th century, gardens tended to grow even larger as their social prestige heightened. The dominating influences in the gardens of overt royalists came largely from France where the magnificence of the royal gardens emphasized the triumph of man over nature or, as many people came to believe, the triumph of king over people.

A new range of building materials encouraged the creation of additional features. The parterre, a flat terrace normally adjacent to the house and laid out with flower beds in regular patterns, became a common feature. The fashion for water as a permanent feature of the garden was expressed in water gardens, ponds and canals. Together with such items as moats and prospect mounds, retained or surviving from earlier days, these features were laid out in a series of small gardens which lay around the house. These were seen as a series of outdoor "rooms". They were still square or rectangular but were separated by hedges or walls so that they could be used in different ways.

Since the gardens of Tudor and Stuart England have left such a poor documentary record locally, we are obliged to recognise their presence from the better known buildings which they accompanied. The years 1570-1640 were a period which W. G. Hoskins saw as the "Great Re-building of Rural England".[17] Elizabethan England saw the prosperity of the nation reflected in the renovation, renewal and building anew of their homes by the richer

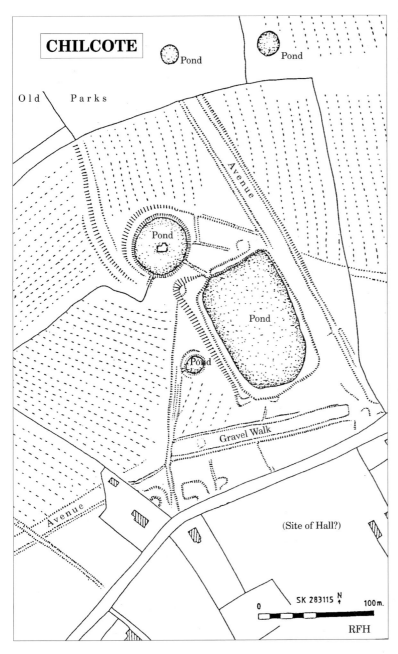

husbandmen, yeomen and lesser gentry. These were the freeholders who shared common origins in the medieval period and who prospered in the entrepreneurial climate of the times.

Fortunately, there is a considerable legacy of remains of these gardens. Indeed, in a few cases, for example *Chilcote*, the surviving earthworks of a former garden are all that remain to point to the existence of an earlier dwelling. More often than not we are left with fragments of these early garden layouts, disturbed by new uses, added to and improved or incorporated piecemeal into new schemes. This is particularly so at *Bradgate* which is described on pages 45–47. Other such remains have often been interpreted in a variety of ways. They have frequently been mistaken for Civil War fortifications and it has only been more recently that their true identities have been recognised.

Elizabethan Gardens

So varied and poorly recorded were the local gardens of the period that it is difficult to group them. Some owners did no more than introduce gradual and seemingly unremarkable changes to their properties, while others were more creative.

Many of the more active men were those whose families had profited from the Dissolution of the monasteries. Francis Cave (d.1584) was one of the King's

30. *Chilcote. The earthworks here are the only remains of what must once have been a substantial hall and its accompanying gardens.*

commissioners for their surrender in Leicestershire and was in a particularly good position to ensure his family benefited. His brother, Brian, acquired *Ingarsby*, the former moated monastic grange of Leicester Abbey, in 1540. Here he built a new house which included part of the original hall. Another brother, Thomas, purchased *Stanford* about the same time and had a house built on the southern bank of the river Avon.

The Noels, another notable Leicestershire family with many branches, acquired the site of *Brooke Priory* where Andrew Noel built a mansion adjacent to what soon became the ruins. He laid out a garden in a complex series of terraces, ponds, parterres and prospect mounds. In 1642 the house ceased to be the principal residence of the family. It fell into disuse and had been demolished by the end of the century. There are some very considerable earthwork remains of these gardens together with an entrance lodge which has survived in part because it has been rather crudely converted into a dovecote.

Another family which profited from the sale of monastic properties was the Beaumonts. John Beaumont of Thringstone bought the site of *Grace Dieu* and converted part of the priory into a

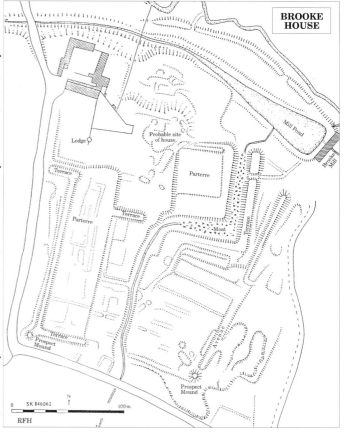

31. *Above: Brooke House, Rutland. A plan of the important earthwork remains of the extensive garden laid out to accompany the Noels' mid Tudor mansion, built adjacent to the site of the Priory of Brooke.*

32. *Left: Brooke House as it was in 1684.*

mansion. Henry Beaumont of *Coleorton* spent large sums from the profits from his coal mines on a new hall and gardens to accompany it. *Stoughton* near Leicester came in marriage via the Farnhams to Henry's brother, Nicholas, who also built a hall. This Elizabethan building was much Gothicised in the 18th century by his descendants, the Kecks, who created extensive new gardens.

The Burtons were an ancient Leicestershire family who had prospered as a result of inheritance, purchase and good management. Sir William Burton, who wrote the history of Leicestershire in 1622, gives as a frontispiece to his great work a drawing of his ancestral home at *Lindley*.[18] This, the earliest published view of a Leicestershire garden, shows a house surrounded by formal gardens laid out in geometrical patterns. They included a knot garden and a parterre which fronted the house. The site was within a moat, the outer perimeter of which was fringed with trees. About 1705 a new house (see p.40) was built on higher ground and part of the ancient moat was filled in and part retained as a garden feature. The last traces of the site were destroyed during remodelling in the nineteenth century.

William Burton's kinsman, Thomas, purchased the manor of *Stockerston* and built a house which may have occupied part of the site of the present Manor Farm. To this day there remains a remarkable collection of the house's formal gardens, terraces, walkways, parterres and fishponds. They extend over both sides of the main street and slope down as far as the Eyebrook.

Other notable and ancient Leicestershire families who were active at this time included the Harpurs of *Hemington*, the Turpins of *Knaptoft* and the Nevills of *Nevill Holt*. One "outsider" was Roger Ratcliffe, an Usher of the Privy Chamber, who married the widow of William Smith of *Withcote*. There he built, very much in the fashion of the times, what Leland regarded as "a right goodly house ... (with) ... the fairest orchards and gardines in those quarters."[19] There are remains of the gardens and terraces in the pastures nearby.

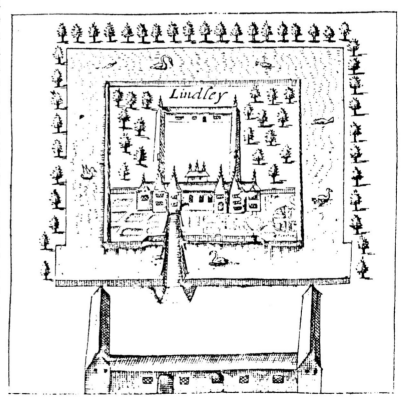

33. *William Burton's House at Lindley c.1622. This is very much a late medieval/early Tudor manor house complete with its moat and small formal gardens.*

Longmate fc

Gardens 1600-1660

Many of the changes and developments in houses and gardens continued into the reigns of the first two Stuarts. Of particular interest in this period is the late flowering of some long established families as knights and substantial country gentlemen. Local farmers too often reached the rank of gentleman and squire and even prosperous yeomen were expressing themselves in the creation of modest houses and gardens.

34. _The manor house of the Burtons at Lindley (see fig. 40) was abandoned in the 18th century in favour of a new building on the hillside above. Parts of the original site, middle right of the picture, were retained as garden features in the new park._

At a lordly level, the Duke of Buckingham created gardens to accompany his new park and grand house at _Burley-on-the-Hill_. A ground plan produced after the Civil War (see fig. 32) shows terraces, a bowling green, a prospect mound and a series of avenues of trees.[20] Some elements survive

Burley-on-the-Hill

When the great mansion was built between 1694 and 1708 for Daniel Finch, Earl of Nottingham, he and his successor, the sixth Lord Winchelsea, created the two great avenues of trees which are still to be seen today . The eastern avenue extends for about a mile (1½ km) from the house, and the southern one for a similar distance to the south. At the end of the eighteenth century Humphry Repton was here and introduced two main changes for its owner, the ninth Earl of Winchelsea. He replaced the brick terraces to the south with a stone terrace, and to the north he opened up the forecourt and redesigned the approaches to the house. Today, the house has been divided into apartments and, appropriately, a small fenced-in area has been stocked with deer.

35. *Above: The south front*

36. *Left: A view looking up the southern avenue of trees towards the great house.*

37. *Right: The map well illustrates the two great formal avenues of trees, extending east and south from the house.*

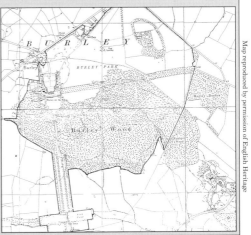

Map reproduced by permission of English Heritage

to the present including a lodge and archway at the end of the south avenue.

Gardens on such a grand scale were the exception rather than the rule. More typical were those laid out to accompany the new manor house of the Brudenells at *Stonton Wyville*. At *Ragdale*, the Shirleys built what Pevsner was moved to describe as "one of the finest 16th-17th century houses in the county".[21] Alas, house and gardens were destroyed in 1958, an act of vandalism sadly typical of that and

38. *Quenby Hall was built in about 1630 by the wealthy Ashby family who owned the entire manor. They had earlier depopulated the village to empark for sheep, leaving the remains to grass over. The formal gardens were laid out to the south of the house, possibly using some of the humps and bumps of the former village.*

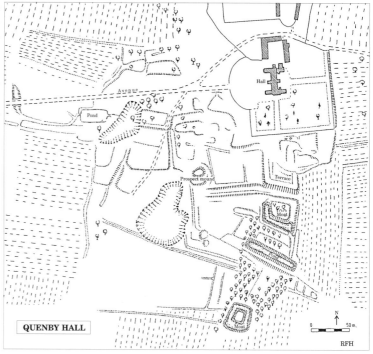

QUENBY HALL

the following decade. At *Quenby*, the Ashbys used some of the earthworks of the village they had depopulated as part of the features of the garden of their new house. The Skipworths' ill-fated mansion at *Cotes*, which was built about 1600 and burnt down less than a century later, has also left an earthwork legacy of garden features.

Along with the plan of *Lindley*, we may also have some idea of the gardens of the times from the drawing of about 1790 of the Wightmans' house at *Burbage*. This rare survivor from a century and a half earlier, included an L-shaped canal, a house on a

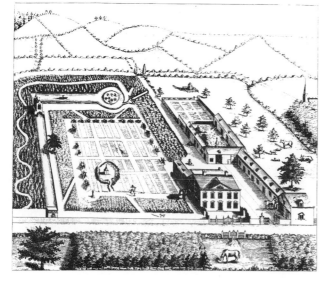

bridge, plantations, winding paths, a parterre with beds of flowers and a bower enclosed by a hedge.[22]

In the early 17th century, *Kirby Bellars Hall* was one of the grandest houses in Leicestershire yet no picture survives to give us an idea of its appearance and no map to allow us to appreciate the great scheme of the gardens. Both were the creation of Sir Erasmus Fontaine, a wealthy and influential man who was High Sheriff of the county in 1628. Although the mansion was burnt down during the Civil War it had been rebuilt by the time of Sir Erasmus' death in 1672. The laying out of the more modest gardens at the former monastic house of

39. *Burbage House c. 1811. This was a rare surviving example of a 17th century manor house with its gardens.*

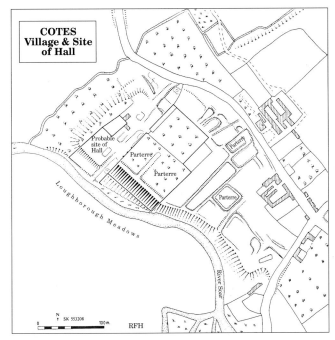

40. *Top Left: Cotes near Loughborough. The extensive earthworks are the remains of the gardens which accompanied the Hall. This was built by the Skipwiths c. 1600 and was destroyed by fire in the 18th century.*

41. *Bottom Left: Aerial view of the site at Cotes.*

42. *Bottom Right: Kirby Bellars Hall. The extensive gardens here in the 17th century were the creation of Sir Erasmus Fontaine.*

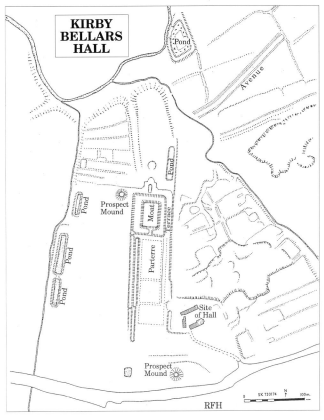

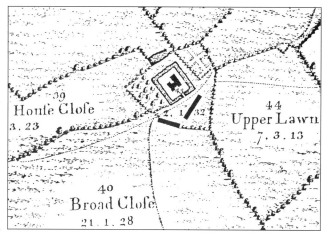

43. *Moated Site at Breedon Lodge Farm 1758. This small but impressive moat, which is still filled with water, surrounded the site of the dwellings of successive keepers of Breedon medieval park. In 1652 the house was described as consisting of 'a hall, a parlour, a kitchen with thirteen other rooms below and above stairs ... which lodge is moated round having a garden and orchard ...'. The last two features are evident from this map.*

little bays of a building, a garden, an orchard and a homestead", all occupying an area of about two acres.[23] The vicarage at *Belgrave*, described thirteen years later as "a mansion house", had a large collection of buildings, an orchard and a garden.[24] John Plumbe of *Potters Marston*, Edward Temple of *Sibson* and Thomas Ward of *Ibstock* were all wealthy yeomen with gardens, orchards and dovehouses.[25]

The Civil War

The tumult and disruption of the Civil War brought to an end many parks. Gardens, too, were destroyed, especially those of royalists by the soldiers of Parliament who regarded them as political statements by their owners. The Cavendish residence by *Leicester Abbey* went up in flames as did the Buckingham mansion at *Burley-on-the-Hill*. The parks and gardens at *Bagworth* and *Coleorton* did not survive Roundhead activities. Lord Huntingdon and the Hastings family paid particularly dearly for backing the losing side: *Burleigh House* at Loughborough was burnt down, their three parks at *Ashby* were destroyed and their *Great Park* at *Loughborough* had to be sold to pay fines. Profiting from the parliamentary ascendancy were such families as the Winstanleys of *Braunstone* and the Packes of *Prestwold* who in turn were later to empark their own estates

44. *Breedon Lodge moat with Lodge Farm 1982.*

Launde and the tiny gardens of the moated site at *Breedon* was probably also carried out before the Civil War.

Wealthy clergymen also had substantial gardens. The vicarage at *Claybrooke* in 1638 had "five bays and a barn of five bays, a stable, two other

The Gardens of Bradgate Park

Bradgate Park, covering some 800 acres, lies five miles north-west of Leicester and contains the ruins of the 16th century mansion of the Grey Family. At the time of its creation, Bradgate House was one of a number of large and imposing country houses which were being constructed in brick in various parts of the country. Whereas the layout and disposition of the rooms at Bradgate conformed pretty much to the fashion of the day, it was distinctive in that it marked the abandonment of the traditional grand gatehouse fronting a totally enclosed court and led the way to the appearance of the truly open, i.e. non-fortified, country house of later years. Subsequent modifications to both house and gardens at Bradgate reflected the aims, ambitions and very varied fortunes of successive generations of the same family.

Bradgate and the Greys

Bradgate Park was a typical small medieval hunting park, first recorded in 1241. Later it was much expanded to cover about 1000 acres. It passed to the Greys by marriage and descended to Thomas Grey (1451-1501). The marriage of his widowed mother to King Edward IV brought him into court circles and he was created Marquis of Dorset in 1475. His son Thomas, the 2nd Marquis (1477-1530), spent much of his life on royal business, including a disastrous military campaign to France. He was succeeded as 3rd Marquis by his son Henry (1517-1554) who in 1535 married Frances Brandon, the niece of Henry VIII. This enhanced high level royal connection brought great wealth and the title Duke of Suffolk. Henry, along with his daughter, Jane (the 'nine day queen'), were executed for treason in 1554. In disgrace, the surviving branch of the family moved to Essex. It is doubtful if Bradgate saw a resident Grey for another 50 years, although Queen Elizabeth undertook to maintain the fabric of the House in return for the right to reside there 'at pleasure'. Eventually, the family fortunes recovered and Suffolk's nephew Henry (?-1614) as lord Grey of Groby, moved the family back to Bradgate early in the 17th century. His son, yet another Henry (c.1600-1673) was created earl of Stamford in 1628 and entertained Charles I at Bradgate in 1634. However, during the Civil War he was an active Parliamentary commander, only to change sides for the Restoration of 1660. His successor as 2nd earl was his grandson, Thomas (c.1653-1719), who supported the cause of William of Orange in 1688 and entertained the new monarch at Bradgate in 1690. About 30 years later Harry Grey, the 3rd earl (1685-1739), deserted Bradgate in favour of his mansion at Enville (Staffs). Bradgate fell into decay and was never lived in again. It remains a romantic ruin, now in the care of Leicestershire County Council.

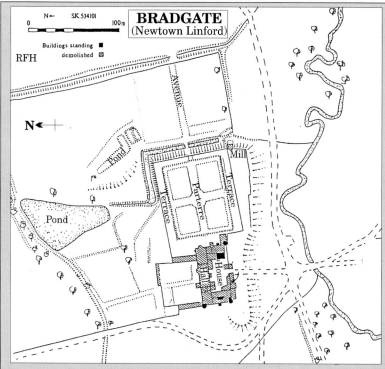

BRADGATE
(Newtown Linford)

45. *Overleaf: Aerial view of the ruins of Bradgate House from the west.*
46. *Left: The plan shows the remains of the walled garden, the raised walkways and sunken parterres to the east of the House.*

It has often been stated that Bradgate House was built largely by Thomas Grey, the 1st Marquis, around 1490 and completed after his death by his son Thomas. There is, however, little evidence to support this view. Since the documentary evidence of any kind for the early 16th century is very slight, an examination of what remains of the house is probably the best we have. It is also important to compare Bradgate with similar and better documented buildings of the same period elsewhere.

The surviving fabric presents a number of problems. In the first place the entire building has been plundered for materials and the remains have suffered greatly from almost two centuries of decay. The upper floors have all but disappeared, with the result that important evidence, especially from the interior roof structures, has disappeared. Moreover, some of the materials have been re-used at different times and, in the present century, have even been incorporated into 'historic' reconstruction of supposed ancient features of parts of the house.

Architectural evidence from the surviving fabric indicates that building at Bradgate was initiated by the 1st Marquis and that most of the House was the work of Thomas, his son. The work was carried out at the same time that he depopulated the village of Bradgate to enlarge the park. It is also likely that Henry Grey, as Duke of Suffolk, continued with further additions and alterations, but that after his death little more than maintenance work took place until the close of Elizabeth's reign. Thereafter, it is also very likely that Henry Grey, lord Groby, brought about much needed modernisation and refurbishment. Additional improvements probably preceded the visits of Charles I and William of Orange. Since arriving at a plan of the House and establishing a chronology for its development is so difficult, accounting for the arrival of the gardens and their evolution is equally hazardous. This is compounded by the fact that the three dominant surviving features: the walled garden, the raised walkways and the sunken parterres could all have been constructed at any time from the first moves by the 1st Marquis to the outbreak of the Civil War. The following seems to offer the best explanation at present:

The first major effort at laying out a garden was carried out by the second Marquis with additions and improvements by his son, Suffolk. Both men used their house for entertaining social equals and suitable gardens would have been essential. If the House was in effect unused by the Greys during the reign of Elizabeth, the gardens would have remained unchanged. Lack of major alterations thereafter would leave us today with a garden which is essentially early Tudor. Such a garden is not what we find. The enclosed rectangular area to the east of the House appears to mark the site of the earliest garden. This however was later redeveloped by Lord Grey on his family's return to Bradgate and his modernisation of the property. Further alterations and additions were probably made by his son, Stamford, around 1630. The rectangular garden retained some of the walls of the Tudor structure but was redeveloped so that the main east-west axis was aligned with that of the House. It was also aligned with a new area of formal garden which extended eastwards and opened on to the wilderness of the Park. The juxtaposition of the House (the centre of civilisation), the garden (the triumph of Man over Nature) and the Park (untamed Nature) was a concept familiar to 17th century gardeners. The addition of further

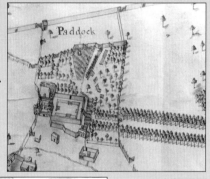

'boxes' of gardens to the north and west, as shown in the drawing by Knyff, the conversion of the leat from the pond into a moat or canal and the arrival of additional formal pools are all features typical of a garden designed before the Civil War. Further development at Bradgate took place for the visit of William III, when temporary stabling was erected. The grand avenue of trees, not shown by Knyff but represented on the later map, was established shortly before the desertion of the House c.1720. So too was the area known as 'the Paddock' which was enclosed from the Park. Thereafter, the House was abandoned for good, although considerable sums were later spent on the upkeep and even improvement of the Park.

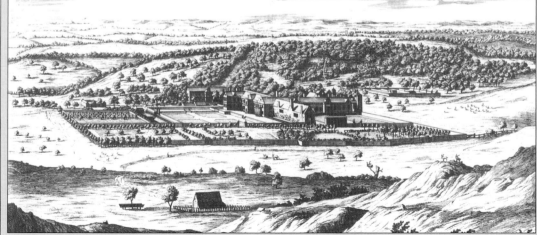

47. *Above: Detail of a map of 1746. Bradgate house and gardens from the south. The avenue of trees leads eastwards across the park.*
48. *Left: Engraving of Bradgate House from the north, by Leonard Knyff, of about 1700.*

CHAPTER THREE
The Grand Design: Parks and Gardens, 1660 – 1750

Following the restoration of Charles II to the throne of England in 1660, the influences upon the design of English parks and gardens came mainly from abroad. Having spent his exile in France, Charles came to admire the work of the great French gardener Andre le Nôtre and, indeed, very soon after he regained the throne Charles invited him to come to England, although there is no record that he ever did so.[1] Nevertheless, the major elements of Le Notre's style of landscape gardening became widely accepted in England in succeeding decades. These included the creation of broad vistas from the house by planting woodland through which carefully placed paths or rides were cut; and by the use of water in the form of moats, canals, pools and fountains. Formal gardens were still created round the house itself in the form of parterres in which low hedging and elaborate coloured flowers and sand were deployed. This was facilitated by the importation from abroad of increasing numbers and varieties of plants.

Another major foreign influence emanated from Holland. While this had been the case to some extent earlier in the seventeenth century, it greatly increased after 1688 when William and Mary ascended to the throne. During their reign, many large gardens were remodelled in the comparatively intimate Dutch fashion. A particularly good example is to found at Hampton Court where the 'privy', or private, garden has recently been recreated along its original lines. The overall effect of these developments was that although formal gardens continued to be made, the concepts upon which they were based spread out from them into the parks beyond so that, in Jane Fearnley-Whittingstall's words, "they leapt the fence".[2]

Formal Parks and Gardens

The features described above were all to be found in a substantial number of parks and gardens created in Leicestershire and Rutland during this period and although they were very largely swept away by the 'naturalistic' park landscapes created by 'Capability' Brown and his followers in the latter part of the eighteenth century, some traces are still visible today. A vivid, if somewhat idealised, picture of how they appeared in their heyday can be obtained from contemporary paintings and drawings. At Belvoir, for example, the old castle buildings having been ruined in the Civil War, a new mansion in the classical style was built in the 1660s and around it were created terrace gardens, avenues and plantations in the grand manner. This highly elaborate formal scheme was completed in the early eighteenth century and, as a painting of 1731 by Thomas Badeslade shows, it was still intact at that time. However, some 20 years later it had largely disappeared and the only feature that remains today

49. *Above: This painting of the south-west prospect of Belvoir Castle in 1731, attributed to Thomas Badeslade, shows the formal gardens that were in existence at this time.*

50. *Below: This hedged area of Belvoir Castle, some 150 metres south of the main building, is all that remains of the late seventeenth century gardens. It contains 7 statues of about 1680 by Colley Cibber.*

is the hedged area some 150 metres south of the castle containing seven statues by Colley Cibber of about 1680. Elsewhere in Leicestershire, remains of formal park landscapes are to be found in a number of places, including Carlton Curlieu Hall, Market Bosworth Hall, Noseley Hall and Stanford Hall. At *Carlton Curlieu,* where the Hall, situated in its own grounds to the south-east of the church, was rebuilt and remodelled several times in the seventeenth century, parts of the contemporary avenues of trees survive, together with a small rectangular moat which was probably a feature of the garden. Around *Market Bosworth Hall,* built by Sir Beaumont Dixie between 1682 and 1692 and now a hotel, two sides of what appears originally to have been a three-sided moat remain, while to the north of the Hall are remnants of fishponds and terraces. At *Noseley Hall,* the ancestral home of the Hazleriggs, rebuilt in the early eighteenth century, the formal plantations and avenues that radiated out from the Hall in the mid-eighteenth century were later swept away and replaced by a 'natural' landscape. However, traces of the formal park landscape remain in the shape of some trees and ponds, earthwork remnants and soil marks. At *Stanford Hall,* in the extreme south of the county,

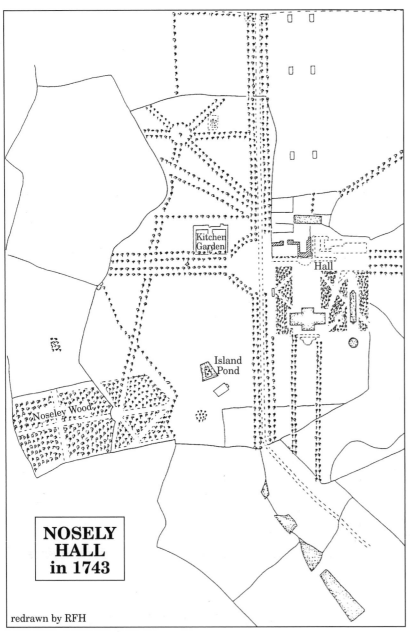

NOSELY HALL in 1743

Kitchen Garden

Hall

Island Pond

Noseley Wood

redrawn by RFH

where extensive formal planting took place in the late seventeenth century, much still remains including the northern double avenue of trees which extends for one-and-a-half kilometres from the Hall and sections of similar avenues to the south, south-west and north-west. Sadly, one of the greatest park and garden landscapes in the county, at *Gopsall*, has vanished virtually without trace. From 1747 onwards, Charles Jennens, a descendant of Humphrey Jennens, ironmaster, who bought Gopsall in 1685, built the hall and developed the park of 1,000 acres. He spent 80,000 pounds on the grounds, an enormous sum at the time, which included walled gardens, terraces, moats and ponds.[3] The park is now farmland, while the house described by Pevsner as "the most expensive and lavishly decorated in the county" was tragically demolished in 1951. Similarly, at *Edmondthorpe Hall* on the Lincolnshire border, the Hall had extensive avenues of trees radiating out from it, to the edges of the parish, but these have all gone. The Hall was burnt out in 1942 and although only fragmentary and overgrown ruins remain, the present owner, Squire Pochin, plans to rebuild it as it was

51. *This plan of Noseley Hall in 1743 shows the formal avenues radiating from the hall. (Redrawn by Robert F. Hartley from an original in the possession of Lord Hazlerigg.)*

52. *Above: This painting of Quenby Hall of c.1740s shows the avenues of trees which extended outwards from either side of the house*

53. *Right: Burley-on-the-Hill from the west. In the centre is the mansion built between 1694 and 1708 for Daniel Finch, Earl of Nottingham. The succession of parks which have been laid out at Burley and which are described in the text occupied that area which is now mostly woodland. The northern edge of another and separate medieval park, Barnsdale Park, (shown on p.14) which was adjacent to Burley, can be seen to the right of the new Oakham to Empingham road, all but flooded by Rutland Water.*

before the fire. At *Quenby*, built for George Ashby in the early seventeenth century and outwardly virtually unchanged, by the early eighteenth century two avenues of trees extended outwards, one on either side of the house, as is well illustrated in a painting dating from the 1640s.

Burley-on-the-Hill in Rutland (figure 53) was also given an extensive formal park landscape in the late seventeenth and early eighteenth centuries. Its owners, Daniel Finch, second Earl of Nottingham (1647-1729) and his successor, the sixth Lord Winchelsea, between them created the two great avenues of trees, which are still to be seen today, and

54. *An engraving of Exton Old Hall, based on Badeslade's painting of 1739*

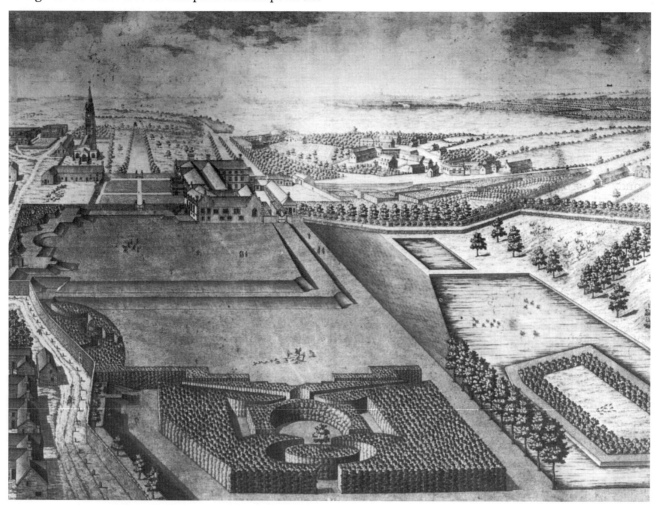

a series of five terraces to the south of the house. It is not known if major landscape designers of the period were involved in these developments.[4] Today, from the centre of the terraces a great avenue of trees leads south for a mile (1½ kilometres) and another grand avenue extends east for a similar distance. The southern avenue ends with a series of flanking pools now cut off from the trees by the Oakham-Stamford road, while the woodland between the avenues, Burley Wood, retains lines of the early eighteenth century rides. The other great historic park in Rutland, *Exton*, was also the site of a major formal reshaping in the late seventeenth or early eighteenth century, for its owner, the Earl of Gainsborough. The painting of 1739 by Badeslade (opposite) shows an extensive geometrical scheme centred on the Old Hall which was burned down in 1810, together with a series of small ponds and lakes. Only the general disposition of some of the ponds and areas of woodland survive the later 'Capability' Brown-style 'naturalisation' of the park. There was another Rutland park at *Tickencote*, where the hall was built by John Vanburgh in

1705 for the Wingfield family. The Hall was pulled down in the 1950s, leaving stables and outbuildings, which have been made into a large house, still in its parkland setting.

As for formal walled gardens, many were to be found around houses in the two counties – at *Bradgate*, for example, which was unusual in escaping formal park landscaping as it did later eighteenth century 'naturalising'. *Staunton Harold* gardens, which also appear in a Kip and Knyff engraving, contained parterres, trees – certainly cherry, peaches, nectarines and mulberries and probably yews and hollies which were popular at the time- topiary, fountains and statues, while beyond the east end of the church was the largest 'canal' in the county.

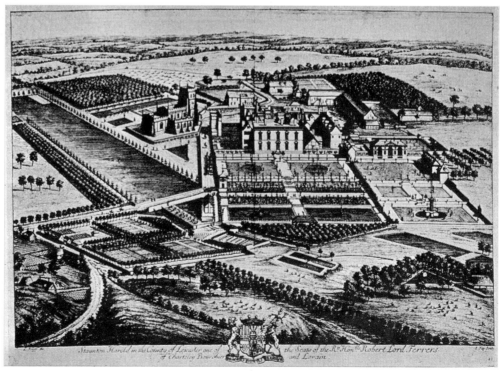

55. *This engraving of Staunton Harold, of about 1716 by Kip, shows the formal gardens and the tree-lined "canal" (middle left of picture),*

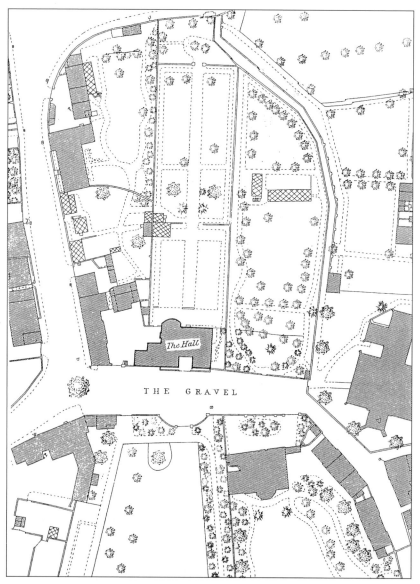

THE GRAVEL

The Hall

56. *Belgrave Hall and Gardens, Leicester. This drawing by Robert F. Hartley shows the consecutive walled gardens and formal flowerbeds which still exist behind the hall.*

Perhaps the best idea of what a formal garden of this sort was like can be obtained today by a visit to *Belgrave Hall,* now a Leicester City museum. Here, a substantial part of the eighteenth century garden remains with its consecutive walled sections and formal arrangements of flower beds. Elsewhere in Leicestershire very little remains: at *Burbage Moat House* where once was a fine formal garden, part of the moat still survives as an earthwork; at *Nevill Holt* a terrace wall with a retaining wall on its north side is all that is left of a once extensive garden; and at *Scraptoft Hall* there is a prospect mound with remnants of terraces and fishponds.

By the first half of the eighteenth century, the Grand Tour had become fashionable for men of wealth and social standing and one of the fashions they brought back from their travels was a desire to create an Italianate landscape with classical park 'furniture'. These 'follies' included temples, arches, obelisks and ruins. Perhaps the best collection in the two counties is to be found in *Garendon Park* whose park monuments designed by Ambrose Phillips between 1729 and 1739 include the Temple of Venus, inspired by the Temple of Vesta in Rome, the Triumphal Arch, a reconstruction of the Arch of Titus (described by Pevsner as "the earliest known representation for its own sake of a

57. *The Triumphal Arch at Garendon Park, erected between 1729 and 1739.*

garden and the park beyond, was important in that it removed the need for walls and opened up the view from the garden. While Bridgeman, who died in 1738, does not appear to have 'improved' any estates in Leicestershire or Rutland, his innovation proved as popular here as elsewhere in the country. While they do not necessarily date back to the early eighteenth century, good examples are to be found at *Blaby Hall,* part of which the District Council plans to turn into a recreational area; at the front of *Donington Hall* where the ha-ha was

triumphal arch in England"), and an 80 feet high Obelisk of rendered brick. The park was also furnished with great avenues of trees but these had been felled and sold off as fuel for iron furnaces by the end of the eighteenth century.

Charles Bridgeman and the Ha-Ha

By the early eighteenth century the formal style of landscaping was already being challenged and the movement towards less formality particularly found expression in the work of Charles Bridgeman (?-1738) who is generally reputed to have first introduced the ha-ha into English gardens. The ha-ha, in effect a ditch strengthened by stone or bricks which marked the boundary between the created in about 1960 by the then owner of the hall and park, Major John Gillies Shields; at *Stanford Hall,* where it is situated beyond the lawn immediately north of the Hall giving views of the main northern avenue; and at *Clipsham Hall* in Rutland where the ha-ha divides the eighteenth century building and its large walled garden from the park. An interesting survival is in the village of *North Luffenham* in Rutland. While the fine Hall still stands in the village, its park has disappeared and its semi-circular stone-walled ha-ha, which once allowed uninterrupted views from the gardens of the Hall across the parkland, now stands at the end of the lawn in front of the village hall.

CHAPTER FOUR
Parks and Gardens in the Later Eighteenth Century

Lancelot 'Capability' Brown (1716 – 1783)

Even when formal park and garden landscapes were at their most popular, in the late seventeenth and early eighteenth centuries, there were the beginnings of a movement against formality and an "irregular" school of landscape design began to appear.[1] This movement was fostered by a number of writers such as Joseph Addison and Alexander Pope who advocated a more "naturalistic" approach to landscape design. However, the "triumph of naturalism", as it has been termed,[2] had to wait until the latter part of the eighteenth century with the arrival on the scene of Lancelot Brown. Known as "Capability" Brown because he constantly averred that the landscape had great "capabilities of improvement", he dominated landscape design in the second half of the eighteenth century and it is to him and his followers that we owe much of the familiar park landscape of England today.

Born in Northumberland in 1716, Brown came to Stowe in Buckinghamshire in 1740 where he worked under William Kent, a celebrated architect and landscape designer who died in 1748. Eleven years later, he left to set up his own consultancy in London. Soon acquiring many wealthy and aristocratic clients, over the next 30 years he came to dominate landscape design, becoming the most famous designer of his time and, in all, "improved" some 180 parks and gardens all over the country. Moreover, he developed a style of landscape design which could be copied reasonably easily by professionals and amateurs alike, so that his influence on the park landscape spread far and wide.

The core of his philosophy was his determination to sweep away the formal landscape of the time and replace it with one which "conceived the ground as a kind of undulating green canvas on to which sunlight could trace complex patterns of light and shade".[5] Among the major features of his style were sweeps of grass which came up to the house, adapting the design to the existing contours of the ground, diverse groups of trees, continuous panoramic views with a winding river in the centre spanned by a bridge, lakes, and vistas with classical "furniture" as their focal points. This "naturalistic" style in many cases involved a vast expenditure of money, requiring among other things the shifting of huge amounts of earth and the planting of great numbers of trees. By the latter part of the eighteenth century, this type of park was becoming a status symbol and a wealthy class was growing which could afford to build country houses and set them in landscaped parks. And so, an "extraordinary consensus" developed,[4] and in Leicestershire and Rutland, as almost everywhere else in the country, many "naturalistic" parks were created, either by sweeping away their formal predecessors or by starting from scratch. The products of this movement still characterise much of the parkland in the two counties. As for 'Capability' Brown himself, he appears to have designed only one park in the area, at Stapleford in Leicestershire where his foreman was busily employed in 1775. Although he also visited Belvoir Castle at one time, there is no evidence that his talents were deployed there.

However, many other landowners employed his followers or used their own skills to devise landscapes in his style, and Leicestershire and Rutland have many excellent examples. These range from large estates to smaller country houses surrounded by their own small areas of parkland. Among the most characteristic larger late eighteenth century parks in the two counties are Exton, Garendon, Lowesby, Prestwold, Quenby, Stanford, Stapleford and Staunton Harold.

Exton Park in Rutland now contains about 240 acres (100 hectares) of parkland; at its most extensive when landscaped in the eighteenth century it contained no fewer than some 1700 acres (700 hectares). The present park lies on fairly level ground, mainly to the south and west of Exton Hall. It contains woodland and scattered mature trees, with a stream flowing through it feeding a series of streams or ponds, including a large main lake which is backed by woodland. It has on its eastern shore Fort Henry, a very pretty Gothick summerhouse of 1785-90. At *Garendon*, the early eighteenth century park was created for its owner, Ambrose Phillips, presumably at the time when he built a new house to replace the existing seventeenth century one. At

58. *Exton Park, a typical Capability Brown-style landscape. In the distance is Fort Henry, a Gothick summerhouse of the late eighteenth century.*

its most extensive it was about 720 acres (300 hectares) in size, but it has since been much reduced. A lake, partly silted up, and belts of trees and small areas of woodland remain, but the most noteworthy features of the park, already referred to, are the monuments and buildings including the Temple of Venus, the Triumphal Arch and the Obelisk. At *Lowesby,* the parkland is mainly open grassland with some scattered mature trees and a belt of woodland which encloses 2 ponds. In the parkland is the site of the deserted village of Lowesby. At *Langton Hall,* 4 miles to the north of Market Harborough, some 50 acres (21 hectares) of the later eighteenth century park remain. The park, originally larger, is thought to have been landscaped by the Reverend William Hanbury who became Rector of nearby Church Langton in 1753. Radiating from the Hall, built in the 1660s and given a "Gothicised" front in 1802, are three avenues of lime and oak, while to the west of the house is an extent of parkland, containing mature trees, which commands a magnificent view over the undulating Leicestershire countryside. *Prestwold* has been altered since its eighteenth century parkland was created so that details of the original landscaping are uncertain. However, the park includes a line of cedars of Lebanon to the east of the hall and woodland with fine mature trees to the west.

As we have seen, 'Capability' Brown was active at *Stapleford Park* where in 1775 he drew up a scheme of landscaping. The scheme was realised and, in John Antony's words, "here are the perimeter belts and clumps of trees, the lake of sinuous outline and the rounded, gently rolling landscape which are so characteristic of Brown in the full flood of his career."[5] (see fig. 28). *Staunton Harold* is a good example of a park created by the landowner himself, albeit doubtless with professional help. In the 1760s, the fifth Earl Ferrers, who also enlarged and remodelled the Hall, "naturalised" the previously formal landscape by creating sweeps of grassland and two artificial lakes. Another park created about this time was *Normanton* in Rutland, for its owner Sir Gilbert Heathcote, a city merchant and a founder and Director of the Bank of England. In order to make the park, surrounding his great house, the parish was depopulated in about 1764, the church and village demolished, and the villagers rehoused in Empingham. The house which had been built some 30 years earlier was altered and enlarged at about the same time as the park was created. The house was demolished in 1925 but the park remained; in the 1930s it was described as being well-timbered and extending over 400 acres (166 hectares).[6] It disappeared under Rutland Water in the 1970s. Finally, mention should be made of the park at *Gumley* where in 1764 Joseph Cradock, a friend of Dr Johnson and Garrick, had the hall built and laid out the gardens and plantations along the lines of the Parc St Cloud in France. The park provided fashionable pleasure grounds and, in the summer, was visited by the gentry of Leicester who came particularly for the mineral waters of its "spa", a chalybeate spring found in 1789.[7] Although, sadly, the Hall was demolished in 1964, much of the park remains with woods and lakes and the earthworks of the formal gardens are still evident.

Of the smaller parks in Leicestershire, created or remodelled in the later eighteenth century, reference should be made to Baggrave, Braunstone and Nevill Holt. *Baggrave Hall* dates from the sixteenth century, but was largely rebuilt in the 1750s. It is set in beautiful, mainly open, parkland which extends for 163 acres (68 hectares). To the west of the Hall is the Prince of Wales Covert, planted in the early twentieth century to commemorate the visit of the Prince of Wales, later King Edward VII, and to the north is an artificial lake bordered by a water garden of about 1900. In the southern part of the park is the site of the village, deserted in the early sixteenth century. *Braunstone Hall* was designed in 1776 as a gentleman's residence for the Winstanley family. Set on rising ground, a position favoured at that time, it overlooks the surrounding parkland. In 1925, the estate was purchased by the then Borough of Leicester largely for housing and nearly 168 acres (70 hectares) were set aside as a public park to serve the housing estate. *Nevill Holt Hall* dates from the fourteenth century when it was a manor house. Subsequently, it was remodelled and extended, especially in the nineteenth century by the Cunard family. Having passed through various hands it has been a private school since 1919. In the later eighteenth century, the house was surrounded by a considerable extent of parkland, replacing its previously formal park and gardens. A carriage avenue of trees was planted at this time of which some still remain. *Scraptoft Hall* in its present form dates largely from the early eighteenth century. The park was laid out by James Wigley, the Leicester MP, and by the end of that century it covered about 100 acres (42 hectares). Now part of de Montfort University, most of the landscaped grounds remain.

Inevitably, just as some parks were created during this period so others were disparked. *Martinsthorpe House,* in Manton, Rutland, the former seat of the Earls of Denbigh, is a good example. Built about 1622, it was a magnificent mansion set in a park. The house was demolished in 1755 when then, or earlier, the park ceased to be maintained. Only the stables were left, subsequently converted into a house, known today as Old Hall

59. *Braunstone Hall was designed in 1776 for the Winstanley family and set in parkland. The estate was purchased by the then Borough of Leicester in 1925, mainly for housing, and 150 acres (70 hectares) were set aside as a public park.*

Farm. Another Rutland park which may have disappeared during the eighteenth century was at *Brooke* where the Noel family built a mansion after the Dissolution. Both *Brooke* and *Martinsthorpe* are shown as being surrounded by parkland on Joseph Wright's map of 1684, but neither is shown on Cary's map of the county in 1792.

Humphry Repton

The immediate successor to 'Capability' Brown as a major force in landscape design was Humphry Repton (1752 – 1818). Although working essentially in the Brown tradition, Repton differed from him in some important respects, introducing modifications

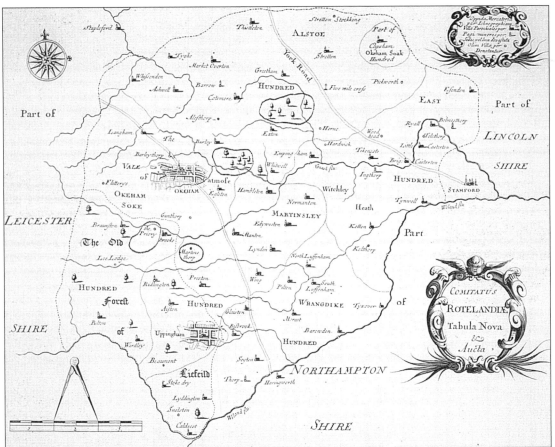

60. *Joseph Wright's 1684 map of Rutland shows the four major parks in the county at that time: Burley-on-the-Hill and Exton, which still exist, and Martinsthorpe and Brooke which have long since disappeared.*

in the "Picturesque" style of landscape design that developed at the end of the eighteenth century. Thus, he concerned himself not merely with the house and its immediate surroundings, but with the whole estate, including opening up views from the house to the horizon. One of his most significant modifications was the re-introduction of the balustraded terrace immediately by the house as a transition between the building and the "natural" park landscape, with, variously, parterres, conservatories, and trellis-covered walks. As part of his concern with the actual site of the park, Repton advocated the planting of trees to follow downwards the line of hills in order to preserve a natural effect.

At least three estates in the two counties were "improved" by Repton: Donington Hall, in north-west Leicestershire, in 1790, and Burley-on-the-Hill in 1795 and Normanton in 1797, the last two both in Rutland. Repton was in the habit of presenting his proposals in the form of a "Red Book" which included watercolours of the landscape both before and after his improvements; those for

61. *This water colour by Humphry Repton, produced for the Earl of Moira in 1790, shows the design by William Wilkins for the new Donington Hall that was shortly to be built in Repton's parkland.*

Burley and Normanton still survive. At *Donington,* the hall was built between 1790 and 1793, in the style of Strawberry Hill Gothick, for Francis Rawdon Hastings, second Earl of Moira and first Marquess of Hastings, to the design of William Wilkins who was introduced to Hastings by Repton. The park extends southwards from the hall, now the headquarters of British Midland Airways, over the undulations of three green valleys; however, of the landscape modified by Repton only the pleasure grounds remain and they are in need of restoration. At *Burley-on-the-Hill*, in 1795-9, Repton introduced two main changes for its owner, the Ninth Earl of Winchelsea: to the south of the house he replaced the previous five brick terraces with a single stone terrace; and to the north he opened up the forecourt and redesigned the approaches to the house to maximise their dramatic impact. At *Normanton*, he redesigned the park landscape which ran northwest from the house across gently rising land. Sadly, little remains today: the eighteenth century house was pulled down in 1925, though the stables still survive, and the park itself is almost entirely submerged under Rutland Water. Another estate which Repton surveyed and for which in 1793 he produced one of his famous "Red Books" for its owner, Sir William Manners, is *Buckminster Hall* and Park, out on the Lincolnshire border towards Grantham. When the original hall was built in the 1790s it was set in a park of 230 acres (100 ha.), of which a portion remains as executed. The original hall was demolished in about 1946 and a smaller building was put in its place.[8]

CHAPTER FIVE
Nineteenth Century Parks and Gardens

In the previous chapter we saw that Humphry Repton was an exponent of the "picturesque" school of landscape design which concerned itself with the whole estate and not merely the house and its immediate surroundings. His modifications of 'Capability' Brown's principles were carried further at the turn of the century in the writings of Sir Uvedale Price and Richard Payne Knight, two Herefordshire squires and intellectuals, who asserted that architectural harmony with the landscape should be the prime object, and that a painter-architect should be responsible for the siting and setting of buildings.[1] In other words, that which was picturesque should be "paintable" and, moreover, should be wild and rugged.[2] A fine example of the picturesque school of landscape design is to be found at *Coleorton Hall* to the east of Ashby-de-la-Zouch. Here, between 1804 and 1808, the hall was built for Sir George Beaumont by George Dance, on the site of an earlier building and the grounds were laid out following advice from Uvedale Price himself, a friend of Beaumont's. Also involved was the poet William Wordsworth who stayed at the house in 1806 and designed the Winter Garden in a disused quarry 100 metres south-east of the hall. In the Winter Garden is a shell grotto designed by Dorothy Wordsworth, the poet's sister. Other remains of the original park are the Rose Garden to the east, later modernised, which is set below a ha-ha to allow an unimpeded view of Bardon Hill; and to the east and north-east the Yew Walk and the Lime Walk, with busts of celebrated writers and artists including Shakespeare, Milton, Michaelangelo and Raphael.[3] Another estate originally laid out on "picturesque" lines is *Whatton House,* at Long Whatton, near Kegworth. The house was built in 1802 by the architect John Johnson for its then owner Edward Dawson and extensively remodelled after a fire in 1876. The park, which was laid out at the time the first house was built, is now farmland though there are scattered mature trees and woodland along the western boundaries. To the south of the house are formal gardens, created after 1876, though the kitchen garden probably dates from about 1802. These gardens are of considerable interest, especially the Chinese Garden with numerous Chinese objects and wrought iron Art Nouveau gates. Two other nineteenth century parks and houses are *Great Glen Hall,* 10 miles south-east of Leicester, set in a small park and *Ayston Hall,* in Rutland, where the northern part of the village was cleared to make way for the park.

A number of new houses and parks were created or substantially modified in subsequent decades. Typical of them are *Quorn House* and *Swithland Hall,* in Leicestershire: the former was built in about 1820 and is surrounded by an area of open parkland which incorporates part of what was the medieval park; and the latter , also in parkland, was completed over several decades after the old hall was burnt down in 1822. Also in the county to the east of Ashby, is *Grace Dieu Manor,* set in its park encompassing the ruins of the former priory; like Quorn Hall, it too incorporates part of the former medieval park. The

Manor, which was built in a Tudor-Gothic style by William Railton for Ambrose Lisle March Phillips in 1833-4, now houses a preparatory school. The site includes ancient woodland, an overgrown walled garden and a gazebo, as well as unidentified earthworks and industrial archaeological features. Currently, there are proposals to open parts of the site to the public. Finally, at *Beaumanor,* near Woodhouse Eaves, where there had been a medieval hunting park and a later Georgian mansion and landscaped park, the house was demolished and a large Victorian mansion erected in 1845 to 1847. Much of Beaumanor park is, at the time of writing, occupied by the Ministry of Defence, while the hall and its grounds are in the keeping of Leicestershire County Council.

Victorian Parks and Gardens

As Franklin has observed,[4] so much landscaping had taken place in the previous century that after about 1840 few Victorian country houses were created from untouched or agricultural land. Instead, existing estates were remodelled. However, most of the alterations that took place were in the immediate vicinity of the house rather than in the outer park and were characterised by a return to formality. Gardens, in particular were transformed by the flood of exotic trees, shrubs and plants which came into the country , brought back by explorers and botanists from all over the world. Conifers, rhododendrons, laurels, monkey puzzles, azaleas, roses and the vast majority of the flowering shrubs we grow nowadays were all introduced.[5] Among the brilliantly coloured bedding plants that were now available from far-flung countries were scarlet pelargoniums and blue lobelias from South Africa and purple verbenas and yellow calceolarias from South America.[6] The display of these trees, shrubs and plants became the prime consideration and as many of them needed environments not greatly different from their native habitats, elaborate rockeries, ferneries and water courses were created to provide the right setting. Improvements in glasshouses made it possible to rear tender plants and foliage to supply the flower beds and parterres with the coloured carpet bedding which the Victorians loved so much. To show off the roses to their best advantage, rose gardens, rose beds, rose arbours, pillars and pergolas were all created.[7]

Perhaps the best example of a Victorian remodelling of the gardens and park took place at *Belvoir Castle* where in the middle of the century the influential head gardener, William Ingram, encouraged by the Duchess of Rutland, wife of the fifth Duke, created the "Duchess's Garden". Some half a mile away from the castle, occupying a natural

62. *Prestwold Hall, rebuilt between 1842 and 1844, sits in its parkland.*

hollow and extending over some five acres, it comprised a mixture of alpines, spring flowers and trees. Redeveloped as a "wild garden" about 1900, it now contains bulbs, spring-flowering shrubs and mature trees. Another good example of Victorian remodelling can be seen at *Prestwold Hall,* outside Loughborough. Here, between 1842 and 1844, when the house was rebuilt and enlarged, major modifications to the eighteenth-century landscape were introduced, including a broad terrace scheme south of the hall and a formal garden arrangement which now includes symmetrical lawns and herbaceous borders. The Victorians were also fond of topiary and perhaps the best example in the two counties is to be found at *Clipsham Hall,* in Rutland, where the famous Topiary Avenue's yews, already in existence, were clipped in the 1870s and 1880s into a variety of shapes.

Kitchen Gardens

By the latter part of the nineteenth century, virtually every large country house had its own walled kitchen garden. Frequently built to a standard pattern and situated relatively unobtrusively some distance behind the house, it varied in size from 2 to 6 acres (0.8 to 2.4 hectares) and was surrounded by tall, red brick walls some 9 feet high, surmounted by heavy, flat stone copings. It was typically divided into four central quarters by gravel paths and surrounded by broad borders alongside the walls. On the south-facing wall would be a long, heated greenhouse. The kitchen garden was intensively cultivated to produce a wide range of fruit and vegetables to feed the owner's family and his servants and vast numbers of bedding plants and flowers for the house and gardens. In the borders along the walls would be espalier and fan-trained fruit bushes.[8] Clearly, kitchen gardens were labour intensive and required a relatively large staff of gardeners to operate them fully. Inevitably, those that remain today and are still in use have to manage with relatively few staff and so

63. *Staunton Harold. In the foreground sits the lake created in the latter part of the eighteenth century, just beyond it is the chapel built in the 1650s, and beyond that the Hall greatly remodelled in the 1760s.*

are less intensively cultivated. Good examples in various states of use and wholly or partially complete are to be found at Exton, Noseley, Prestwold, Quenby, Stapleford and Whatton Hall.

However, if during the latter part of the century, major changes were taking place in the areas immediately around the country houses, the parks beyond were much less altered, and remained much as they had been before. Many of them contained large herds of deer. In his book, "English Deer Parks", published in 1867, E. P. Shirley includes lists of contemporary deer parks. In Leicestershire, these comprised *Bradgate* with about 500 deer, mostly fallow; *Garendon* containing about 1,500 acres (680 ha.) and a herd of 300 fallow deer; *Donington* with a herd of both fallow and red deer; *Staunton Harold* containing 129 acres (58 ha.) with a herd of 230 fallow deer, all black; *Gopsall* with 500 acres (230 ha.) and 264 fallow and 15 red deer; and *Croxton* with 570 acres (260 ha.) and a herd of 350 fallow deer. In Rutland, *Exton* Park contained 800 acres (360 ha.) and 400 fallow deer; and *Normanton* 700 acres (320 ha.) and about 500 fallow deer.[9] Twenty five years later, Whitaker in his book on parks records all the above Leicestershire parks as containing herds of deer of various sizes and, in addition, lists *Stanford Hall* with 165 acres (75 ha.) and 150 fallow deer; and *Stapleford* with 919 acres (417 ha.) and 50 fallow deer.[10]

64. *The reconstructed remnants of Leicester Abbey, founded for Augustinian canons in 1143, were incorporated into the public park, 50 years after its opening in 1882.*

Public Parks

During the latter part of the nineteenth century another type of park, the public or municipal park, appeared. As, following the Industrial Revolution, the cities expanded and became overcrowded, so town councils established urban parks in order to provide some open spaces for the recreation of the people living in them. These were created mainly from about the 1880s onwards and took various forms, depending upon their origins. As one would expect, Leicester, being by far the biggest town in the two counties, has the most parks and, indeed, was the first to establish them, a practice which has continued ever since. As a consequence, Leicester today has over 2,700 acres of parkland and open spaces which are free and open to the public to enjoy. Four late Victorian parks were created in the city, namely Abbey Park, Victoria Park, Spinney Hill Park and Western Park. Although a number of small

Abbey Park

Abbey Park, near the centre of Leicester, is a particularly interesting example of a late Victorian park. Opened in 1882 by the Prince (later Edward VII) and Princess of Wales, an event commemorated by a fine plaque (fig. 65) at

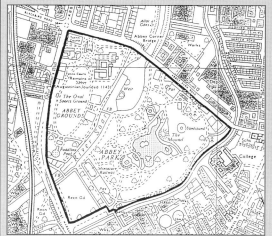

the entrance to the park, it comprises 66 acres of land in the fields surrounding the former site of Leicester Abbey. In addition to the River Soar which flows through it and is spanned by a fine bridge, it contains a boating lake and a wildfowl lake. The portion to the west of the river, Abbey Grounds, was added to the park in 1932 and contains the reconstructed ruins of the Abbey, what is reputed to be Cardinal Wolsey's grave and the ruins of Cavendish house, a late Elizabethan building, burnt down during the Civil War.

65. *The plaque commemorating the opening of Abby Park by the Prince and Princess of Wales in 1882.*

Map reproduced by permission of English Heritage

66. *Above: This map of Abbey Park shows the original Victorian park bounded on the east by the Grand Union Canal and on the west by the River Soar, to which were added the Abbey Grounds in 1932.*

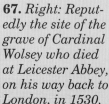

67. *Right: Reputedly the site of the grave of Cardinal Wolsey who died at Leicester Abbey, on his way back to London, in 1530.*

68. *Left: The ruins of Cavendish House, in the northwest corner of Abbey Park, built about 1600 from the remains of the Abbey and burnt out in 1645.*

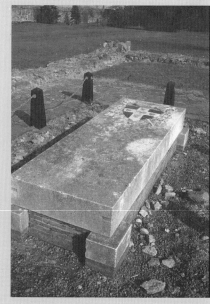

69. *The River Soar flowing through Abbey Park.*

recreation grounds had been opened in the previous forty years, it was not until 1882 that the first public park, *Abbey Park*, was opened, by the Prince of Wales and Princess Alexandra. There is a fine Victorian plaque on a gate pillar at the entrance of the park in commemoration of the event. The park, which lies between the River Soar and the canal, was made from the Abbey Meadows, land that belonged to Leicester Abbey until its dissolution in 1537. Subsequently, in 1932, the Abbey Grounds, containing the few remnants of the Abbey, were added to the park. It is in this latter area that the memorial to Cardinal Wolsey, who died at the Abbey in 1530 on his way to London from York to answer a charge of treason, is to be found. Among other interesting features in the park are the impressive ruins of Cavendish House, built about 1600 from the remains of the Abbey and burnt down in 1645 by Royalist troops during the Civil War, two lodges by James Tait and an artificial lake.

Victoria Park, named of course after Queen Victoria, was the next Leicester park to be opened, in 1883. Until then it had been a racecourse, which was thereupon removed to its present site in Oadby. It contains 69 acres of open parkland, dominated by the war memorial, designed by Sir Edwin Lutyens and erected in 1923. Lutyens also designed the lodges which date from 1933.

Spinney Hill Park was opened in 1885, created from farmland purchased for this purpose, on condition that the timber it contained was to remain. Indeed, it was supplemented by beech and yew trees planted soon after it opened. Today, it contains 34 acres of sloping parkland,

70. *Above: Victoria Park, Leicester. Formerly the site of a racecourse, it was opened as a public park in 1883*

71. *Right: This aerial view of Spinney Hill Park, Leicester, well illustrates its 34 acres of sloping parkland and old trees embedded in the urban landscape.*

together with its spinney of old trees. *Western Park,* which was opened in 1899, was originally outside the borough of Leicester and did not come into the city until the boundary changes of 1935. Comprising 178 acres, it is the largest Leicester park and the most natural in appearance. Much of the land, originally farmland, has remained virtually unchanged since it was opened a century ago and includes open parkland, spinneys and hedgerows as well as a considerable area of playing fields. It also contains a great oak of considerable antiquity which may have been growing when the area was enclosed from Leicester Forest in 1526.

Among the Register of gardens and parks of special interest compiled a few years ago by the Historic Buildings and Monuments Commission and issued by English Heritage, is *New Walk,* in Leicester. Although an urban public walk, or promenade, rather than a garden, it is of particular interest. Laid out by the Corporation in 1785, planted with trees and shrubs provided by public subscription, it was originally known as Queen's Walk. It extends for some 1,100 metres and was developed in the nineteenth century with residences and public buildings. Designated a Conservation Area in 1969, considerable repair and improvement to property have taken place and trees have been replanted. Consequently, its character has been preserved and it has remained a promenade. In Pevsner's words, "it is unique to England in this respect, for it is right in the middle of the town and yet has resisted the intrusion of wheeled traffic. One can still walk unharassed under the trees".[11]

Outside of Leicester, another late Victorian park is to be found, in Loughborough. *Queen's Park* was created on a 4 acre site to mark her Diamond Jubilee in 1897, though it was not opened until two years later. Subsequently, in 1908, the Council acquired another 6 acres to add to the park. It is in many ways typical of its kind with extensive ornamental planting in the form of flower beds, extensive lawns, a variety of trees and a serpentine pond. It also acquired an octagonal bandstand to commemorate the 1902 coronation of King Edward VII and Queen Alexandra. Perhaps its most notable feature is the Carillon, built as a war memorial after the First World War, the first of its kind in the country. It stands 151 feet high, houses a clavier, or musical keyboard, a chamber where the carilloneur plays, a war memorial museum, and a belfry with 47 bells. With its copper-clad roof, it is a major landmark in the town.

72. *Queen's Park, Loughborough, with its lawns, ornamental flower-beds, shrubs and trees and its 151 feet high carillon.*

CHAPTER SIX

Parks and Gardens in the Twentieth Century

The present century has witnessed enormous changes in the management and, indeed, in the very existence of the counties' landscaped parks. One major factor in this process was already becoming evident in the last two decades of the nineteenth century when, from 1879 onwards, the importation of cheap grain from the United States and Russia reduced the value of land in this country to such an extent that in the south of England, for example, rent rolls fell by 40 per cent between the late 1870s and the end of the century. Land prices dropped by a third, and as a consequence, the economic base upon which the great estates had survived was seriously undermined.[1] Their financial position was made worse by the increasing toll of death duties, which rose from 8 per cent in 1904 to 50 per cent in the 1930s, and by the fearful loss of younger males of the landed classes in the First World War. As a consequence, many landowners had to sell their houses and parks, some of which were demolished and lost forever, while others passed into the hands of public and other bodies such as the local authorities and the National Trust. In Leicestershire, for example, Gopsall Hall, which lasted for 200 years, has gone completely, while others like Bosworth Hall, Coleorton Hall, Donington Hall and Quorn Hall have passed out of the hands of the families who owned them. Similarly, in Rutland, Normanton has almost entirely disappeared, while Burley is now divided up into separate apartments.

However, at the turn of the century, these developments were still some way ahead and country houses and parks were still very much in use and, indeed, a few were being built and others modified and extended. One of the last great houses to be built in the two counties was *Papillon Hall,* at Lubenham, west of Market Harborough. Built between 1902 and 1904 for its owner by the distinguished architect, Sir Edwin Lutyens, it was, in Pevsner's words, "lamentably short-lived", being demolished in 1950.[2] It was further distinguished by having a garden planted by Gertrude Jekyll in 1903. Lutyens and Jekyll also combined to create the garden at *Lowesby,* east of Leicester, where the former designed the stables in 1910. He also worked at *Brooksby Hall,* north-east of Leicester. The core of the hall dates from the seventeenth century, but it was much remodelled and extended in the late nineteenth century, when extensive walled gardens were laid out,[3] and again in the early twentieth century, the latter work being done by Lutyens. Alongside the lake in the park is a fine stone pergola which is attributed to Lutyens. The Hall passed through various hands, including those of Admiral Beatty who bought it in 1911, before it became the county agricultural college in 1951. Since then, new buildings have been erected for the College, resulting

73. *Brooksby Hall, originally the home of the Villiers family and the county agricultural college since 1951. In the distance in the centre is the hall, which dates from the seventeenth century, to the left are the modern student residences, and to the right St. Michael's church with its early fourteenth century west tower.*

in the disappearance of at least one walled garden, though in compensation others have been restored.

However, if many of the old landed classes, tied to their properties and dependent upon the value of land for their upkeep, suffered acutely from the steep decline in the value of land from the late nineteenth century onwards, many industrialists, merchants, businessmen and professionals prospered from the growing industrialisation of the country. Some of these, like Corahs the hosiery manufacturers and the Goddards, manufacturers of a celebrated plate powder, built themselves houses in the early part of the twentieth century in such new Leicester suburbs as Oadby and Stoneygate, where they are still to be seen.

Their houses were the centrepieces of what Helen Boynton and Grant Pitches in their admirable book[4] call "miniature estates", emulating all the

features of the parks and gardens of the great landowners, but on a small scale. Typically, their gardens were 4 to 8 acres (1.6 to 3.2 hectares) in size and contained "leisure gardens", lakes, rose and herb gardens, and rockeries. One of the best examples is the *Leicester University Botanic Garden,* at Oadby, created from the grounds of four houses built in the early twentieth century and acquired by the University since 1947 for use as student residences.[5] Much of the 16 acre (6 hectare) layout is fairly informal and contains some fine trees that date back to the time when the houses were built on farmland, although most are more recent plantings. There is also a formal area at the north end with a pool and pergolas, and other features include a small arboretum, rock and woodland gardens and extensive glasshouses.

After a relatively quiescent period in the development of urban parks in the first two decades of the twentieth century, the suburban growth of Leicester in the inter-war years led to a demand for the provision of open spaces which, in the form of parks and gardens, became an integral part of urban planning.[6] Consequently, four parks were created in the city's suburbs which were spreading to the south-west, the south and the east. These parks differed from their late Victorian predecessors in being "multipurpose", that is they were designed from the start to include sporting facilities such as football and cricket pitches, tennis courts and bowling greens. The largest of the four, to which we have already referred, is *Braunstone Park,* whose 167 acres (70 hectares) were purchased by the City from the Winstanley family in 1925. The others are *Humberstone Park,* purchased in 1928, whose 20 acres (8 hectares) include gardens, sporting facilities, and a children's play area; *Knighton Park,* purchased from 1937 onwards, whose 78 acres (32. 5 hectares) include shrubberies, a water garden, heather and rock gardens, and sporting facilities; and *Evington Park,* purchased after the Second World War in 1949, whose 44 acres (18 hectares) include a woodland garden and various sporting facilities.[7]

Another Leicestershire town which created an urban park in the inter-war period is Hinckley, whose *Hollycroft Park* was officially opened in 1935 as part of the Silver Jubilee celebrations for King George V and Queen Mary. Consisting of 11 acres (4. 6 hectares), it has retained many of its original trees, subsequently augmented by others, and includes an Arena (a series of lawned terraces linked by footpaths), ornamental shrubberies, and various sporting facilities. Melton Mowbray also has its park in the shape of *Egerton Park* and *Town Park,* two parks effectively joined to form one. Their 38 acres (16 hectares) include an avenue of chestnuts along the southern perimeter and an archway of about 1480, all that survives of the original manor house and relocated here.

In the years between the wars, the majority of country houses and their parks were maintained, though even then, as already noted, there were losses as houses were pulled down and their parks turned over to agricultural land. With the coming of the Second World War, however, the entertaining that had gone on in the houses and their parks and gardens came to an abrupt end. Many of their families and staffs went off to war, their houses were requisitioned by the military for use as headquarters or hospitals, and sections of the parks were ploughed up to grow food.[8] Inevitably, the vast majority of parks and their gardens were neglected for the greater part of the war and became overgrown.

The Postwar Period

In the more than 50 years that have elapsed since the end of the Second World War, the major changes that have taken place in society have inevitably greatly affected our parks and gardens. For one thing, once the war ended park owners could no longer employ the amount of labour that was available, and for another there was the neglect of six years to make up. Despite these and later difficulties, many parks and gardens have survived, though in some cases having passed out of their original owners' hands. All have had to adjust to changed circumstances by, for example, the use of efficient modern park and garden technology and by adopting labour-saving methods such as grassing over elaborate flower beds, planting shrubs and underplanting with ground cover plants.

In the postwar period, country houses in the two counties have suffered a variety of fates. Some, alas, have been demolished; they include Buckminster in 1946, Papillon in 1950, Gopsall in 1951, Ragdale in 1958 and Garendon and Gumley, both in 1964. In most cases, their parks have gone with them, most frequently reverting to agricultural land. Other houses have been taken over by institutions: *Coleorton,* for example, was, until recently a regional

74. *Bosworth Hall, the ancestral home of the Dixie family, built at the end of the seventeenth century and now a hotel. Opposite lies the park which is now a Country Park run by the County Council, on the site of a medieval park.*

headquarters of the Coal Board; since privatisation of the industry, it has passed into other hands and its future is uncertain. Other "institutionalised" houses include *Donington Hall,* headquarters of British Midland Airways; *Launde Abbey,* used as a retreat and study centre by the Anglican diocese of Leicester; *Scraptoft Hall,* a campus of de Montfort University; and *Staunton Harold,* a home run by the Sue Ryder Foundation. At least one major house, *Burley-on-the-Hill,* has been converted into private apartments; interestingly, a small deer park has been created within the larger park, immediately south of the house. Others, like *Market Bosworth* and *Stapleford* have been converted into hotels. Perhaps a majority of estates still remain in private hands, though not always those of their prewar owners,

75. *Burley-on-the-Hill is now private apartments, but still incorporates an enclosure for deer, seen here.*

in leisure activities. To cater for these developments, the government in the 1960s established the Countryside Commission and encouraged local authorities to create "Country Parks", many of them from parks and other areas of land already in their possession. During the past 30 years or so, Leicestershire has created 8 Country Parks: Beacon Hill, Bosworth Battlefield, Bradgate, Broombriggs Farm and Windmill Hill, Burrough Hill, Foxton Locks, Market Bosworth, and Watermead. *Beacon Hill Country Park,* near Woodhouse Eaves, comprises 180 acres (75 hectares) of heathland, bracken, rhododendrons and woodland. The summit of the hill, at 818 feet one of the highest points in Leicestershire, commands fine views, particularly to the north, over Loughborough, and the Trent and Soar Valleys. The *Bosworth Battlefield Country Park,* two miles south of Market Bosworth, is, as the name indicates, on the site of the Battle of Bosworth which took place in 1485. It has 4 miles of field and woodland paths, incorporating the Battle Trails illustrating the encounter, and an extensive Visitor Centre. *Bradgate Park,* as we have seen, has been a park for the better

including Baggrave, Belvoir Castle, Exton, Langton, Lowesby, Noseley, Prestwold, Quenby, Stanford, and Whatton. At *Quenby*, for example, its owner, the Squire de Lisle, has in recent years created a very fine Italian garden. Some of these houses and their parks, like *Belvoir Castle* and *Stanford Hall,* have been opened by their owners to the public and have become major tourist attractions.

Among the major postwar changes have been greatly increased public mobility, with the widespread ownership of cars, and a considerable growth

76. The Battle of Bosworth Country Park, on the site of the Battle of Bosworth which took place here in 1485.

part of 700 years. As a Country Park, it is Leicestershire's most popular, attracting well over one million visitors every year. Its 850 acres (354 hectares) have changed relatively little in appearance over the centuries and comprise a mixture of heath, bracken, grass covered slopes, rocky outcrops and small woodlands. *Broombriggs Farm,* which lies just opposite Beacon Hill Country Park, is a 139 acre (58 hectare) mixed arable and stock farm with an extensive network of footpaths, including a farm trail and riding tracks. Alongside the farm is *Windmill Hill,* approximately 27 acres (11 hectares), with fine views over Charnwood Forest. *Burrough Hill,* some 5 miles south of Melton Mowbray, is one of the highest points in east Leicestershire. Comprising 82 acres (34 hectares) it is crowned by a magnificent Iron Age hill fort and commands very impressive views to the north and east. *Foxton Locks,* on the Grand Union Canal, about three miles north-west of Market Harborough, are not, of course, a park in the conventional sense but a remarkable example of early nineteenth century canal engineering, consisting of a spectacular staircase of 10 locks. *Market Bosworth Country Park* was opened by Leicestershire County Council in 1970. Once part of the park of Bosworth Hall, now a hotel, its 87 acres (36 hectares) are mainly traditional parkland with mature trees, a lake and a stream. Finally, *Watermead Country Park,* which lies in the Soar Valley just north of Leicester, is also not a park in the conventional sense. Part of a former gravel extraction area, it comprises 230 acres (96 hectares) at present being developed by the County and includes a nature reserve, lakes and woodland walks.

In addition to providing Country Parks, local authorities have also set aside other areas as public leisure and recreation areas. In Leicester, for example, *Riverside Park* is a 12-mile linear park running alongside the River Soar in its course through the city. Developed in stages since 1974, its 2,400 acres (1,000 hectares) include 20 miles of walks, bridleways and cycle paths, as well as some fine examples of the city's industrial archaeology. In the words of Nash and Reeder, it is "a unique urban development, combining ecological, historical and recreational interests".[9] The city has also provided small garden areas, including Aylestone Hall Gardens, Castle Gardens, and the Leicester Arboretum. *Aylestone Hall Gardens* are located on the Aylestone Road on the southern side of the city. The Hall, of Tudor origin, though mostly Victorian in appearance following restoration in 1850, is situated in a small 5-acre (2 hectare) garden with a fine collection of dwarf conifers and herbaceous borders. *Castle Gardens* is on the site of the former Leicester Castle, of which some of the medieval walls remain, overlooking the banks of the River Soar in the centre of the city. It contains a statue of Richard III, commemorating his burial nearby after the battle of Bosworth, a rock garden and mixed borders. *Leicester Arboretum* is situated in Shady Lane, Evington, in the south east of the city. Since it was founded by Leicester City Council, over 300 different varieties of trees have been planted there. Hinckley, like Leicester, has converted the greater part of its castle site into a garden, in this case the *Hinckley Garden of Remembrance.* In the centre of the former castle mound is a bronze figure on a pedestal, poised in the act of benediction. Finally, Leicestershire County Council has acquired and set aside as a picnic area 12 acres of open grassland in the park of *Wistow Hall,* 7 miles south-east of Leicester.

In the case of Foxton Locks Country Park and the Riverside Park in Leicester, the term "park" has today a wider connotation than was formerly the case. Indeed, a number of commercial ventures now describe themselves as parks of one sort or another.

Three examples in the two counties are East Carlton Countryside Park and Stoughton Farm Park in Leicestershire, and Rutland Farm Park in Rutland. *East Carlton Countryside Park,* situated near Market Harborough and overlooking the Welland valley, contains 100 acres of countryside and includes walks through native woodland and open countryside. *Stoughton Farm Park,* at Oadby on the south-east side of Leicester, describes itself as "Britain's biggest working Farm Park". Finally, *Rutland Farm Park,* at Oakham, occupies 18 acres (7.5 hectares) of the former *Catmose Park,* which until the 1930s was part of the country estate of the Noel family. First opened to the public in 1981, it contains fine trees, especially oak, pine and fir, as well as rare plants.

The Future of our Parks and Gardens

In recent years, there has been a growing interest in our splendid inheritance of parks and gardens. This is illustrated by the fact that English Heritage has circulated a Register of Parks and Gardens of Special Historic Interest to local authorities and other organisations who have an interest in their conservation. Moreover, Leicestershire County Council has commissioned the Centre for Conservation Studies at de Montfort University to draw up a supplementary Register of Historic Parks and Gardens and we have drawn extensively on both lists in the course of writing this book. Another encouraging development is the recent establishment of a Leicestershire branch of the Garden History Society. Although the English Heritage Register is purely advisory and provides no special statutory protection to the sites included within it, as a result of legislation passed in October 1995 planning authorities are now required to consult English Heritage on planning applications affecting Grade I and Grade II* registered parks and gardens and to consult the Garden History Society on applications affecting all registered sites, irrespective of their grade. It remains to be seen how effective these measures will be in helping to preserve our parks and gardens from untoward development.

Inevitably, the pressures on our landscape generally, of which our parks and gardens are so essential a part, is unremitting, not least because of the demand for millions of new houses that is likely to eventuate in the next decade or so. In addition, the cost of maintenance of our parks and gardens is high: old woodland decays and is expensive to replace, lakes and streams silt up and park and garden monuments are in need of repair. While grants are available in some measure for these purposes, public awareness and support are essential for their preservation. We are fortunate, indeed, in our rich inheritance of parks and gardens which today, thanks to the generosity of owners who are prepared to open them to the public and to local authorities and others who have created and maintained them, are enjoyed by a greater number of people than ever before.

Finally, at the other end of the scale, in terms of size if nothing else, one should not forget the often remarkable achievements of people with modest gardens for whom the great British tradition, indeed passion, for gardening is as strong as ever. This tradition is well reflected in the large number of gardens which are opened to the public each year, often in aid of specific charities.

Appendix

Medieval Parks in Leicestershire

(Numbers refer to the map on page 12)

	Park	*Date and Source of Earliest Reference*	*Ownership Details*
1	Ashby-de-la-Zouch	pre 1270 (LRO 26D53/409)	Alan la Zouch
2	Bagworth	1279 onwards (Nichols 4/2, p989)	Bishop of Durham
3	Barn (= Barrons = Desford)	1298 (Cal IPM Edw I, vol 3, p289)	Edmund, Earl of Lancaster
4	Barrow (= Quorn)	No later than 1135 (Farnham 1930, p17)	Ranulph, Earl of Chester
5	Barwell	1209 (LMVN vol1, p131)	William de Hastings
6	Beaumanor	1295 (Farnham 1912, p65)	Hugh le Despenser
7	Beaumont Leys	c.1492 (VCH Leics IV p447)	The Crown
8	Belton	c1200 onwards (Nichols 3/2, p638)	Thomas de Verdon
9	Belvoir	1306 onwards (PRO Lists & Indices XVIII p86)	William Ross (licence to impark 'Old Park Wood'
10	Bradgate	1241 onwards (Hastings MSS I, p23)	Earl of Winchester
11	Breedon-on-the-Hill	1226 (LMVN vol 5, p67)	Robert de Tatershal
12	Burbage	1266 onwards (Cal. Pat. R 1258-66, p113-7)	Henry de Hastings
13	Burleigh	1330 (PRO Misc Chancery Inqu. p113-7)	Hugh le Despenser
14	Burton Lazars	1322 (Cal. Pat. R 1321-24, p160)	John Hamelyn
15	Cadeby	1279 (one of 3 parks under Market Bosworth)	Richard de Harcourt
16	Castle Donington	1229 onwards (Cal. Close R. 1227-31 p222)	John de Lacy
17	Cold Overton	1226 (LMVN vol 6, p347)	Robert de Tatershal
18	Coleorton	1252 (LMVN vol 2, p65)	William Maureward
19	Croxton Kerrial	before 1199 (Nichols 2/1 p151)	William Parcarius
20	(Old) Dalby	1300 'Ye Park' (John de Woodford's Cortulary)	Prior of Dalby
21	Earl Shilton (= Tooley Park)	1279 onwards (Nichols 4/2 p774)	Earl of Lancaster
22	Evington	1317 (Cal. Pat. R. 1313-17, p691)	Richard de Grey
23	Foston	1285 (LMVN vol 2, p234)	Agnes de Percy
24	Grace Dieu	1306 (Potter p166) (Licence to empark)	Prioress of Grace Dieu
25	Great Easton	1220 (LMVN(MSS) under Bringhurst)	William de Bringhurst
26	Groby	1279 (Potter p106)	William de Ferrers
27	Hinckley (= Seydley Park)	1297 (TLHAS vol 20 1937-38, p306)	Edmund, Earl of Lancaster
28	Kirby Muxloe	1474 (Cal. Chart. R. 1427-1516, p242)	William, Lord Hastings
29	Knipton	1350 'closes called le Park' (Nichols 2/1 p234)	Isabe Avenell
30	Langley	1193-1207 (Nichols, 3/2 p865)	William de Langley
31	Launde	1248 (Cal Pat R.1248, p326)	Prior de Langley (licence to empark)
32	Leicester Abbey	1352 (Nichols 1/2 p262)	Abbot of Leicester
33	Leicester Frith (= Birdsnest Park)	1297 (Nichols 4/2 p783)	Edmund, Earl of Lancaster
34	Loddington	1248 (Nichols 3/1 p303)	Prior of Launde (licence to empark)

Medieval Parks in Leicestershire (cont.)

	Park	Date and Source of Earliest Reference	Ownership Details
35	Loughborough	1230 onwards (Cal. Close R. 1227-31 p341)	Hugh de Despenser
36	Lubbesthorpe	1348 (LMVN vol 5, p262)	William la Zouche
37	Lutterworth	1640 'a close called The Park' (LMVN 2 p243)	IPM of Arthur Faunt
38a	Market Bosworth: Old Park	1232 onwards (Cal. Close R. 1231-34, p48)	Robert de Harcourt
38b	Mkt Bosworth: Southwood Park	1232 onwards (Cal. Close R. 1231-34, p48)	Robert de Harcourt
39	Nailstone	1279 (Nichols 1/1 p.cxvi)	Richard de Harcourt
40	Nevill Holt	1448 (Cal Chart. R. 1427-1516, p100)	Thomas Palmer
41	Newbold Verdon	1360 (Cal. IPM vol 10, p509)	Eliz de Burgo
42	Normanton Turville (= Brokensale)	1279 (in Thurlaston) (Nichols 4/2 p1001)	Radolphus Turville
43	Norton-juxta-Twycross	1305 'an enclosed park' (Nichols 4/2 p849)	Margery de Plessetis
44	Nosely	1278 (Nichols 2/2 p739)	Anketin de Mortivall
45	Owston	1279 onwards (VCH Leics. vol 5, p272)	Abbot of Owston
46	Ratby	1270 (LMVN vol 6, p352)	Earl of Buchan
47	Rothley	1331 (LRO 44'28/196)	
48	Shepshed (= Oakley Park)	1219-64 (Nichols 3/2 p1013)	Earl of Winton
49	Staunton Harold	1324 (LRO 26D53/494)	William de Staunton
50	Stockerston	1609 a close called 'le Parke' (LMVN vol 4,pp354-55)	IPM of John Burton
51	Twyford	1284 (LMVN vol 4, p246)	
52	Whitwick (= Bardon Park)	1270 (Cal. Pat. R. 1292-1301 p560)	Earl of Buchan

Medieval Parks in Rutland

	Park	Date and Source of Earliest Reference	Ownership Details
1	Barnsdale	1269 onwards (VCH Rutland, vol 1. p253)	
2	Burley-on-the-Hill	1206 (VCH Rutland, vol 2, p114)	Henry de Armenters
3	Essendine	1296 onwards (Cal. Close R. 1288-96, p472)	Robert de Clifford
4	Exton	1185 (VCH Rutland, vol 2, p130)	Earl of Huntingdon
5	Greetham	1446 (VCH Rutland, vol 2, p136)	Earl of Warwick
6	Hambledon	1360 (Cal IPM Ed.III vol 10 p527)	William de Bohun
7	Lyddington	Temp. King John (1199-1216) (VCH Rutland vol 2, p191)	Bishop of Lincoln
8	Market Overton	1269 (VCH Rutland, vol 1, p253)	
9	Oakham, Flitteris Park	1250 (Cal. Pat. R. 36, Hen. III, No. 61)	Earl of Cornwall
10	Oakham, Little Park	1300 (Cal. IPM. Ed. I, vol 3, p461)	Earl of Cornwall
11	Ridlington	1238 onwards (Cal. Pat. R. 1232-47, p237)	The Crown
12	Stretton	1291 (VCH Rutland vol 2, p145)	Eleanor, mother of Edward I
13	Whissendine	1143-1219 (VCH Rutland, vol 2, p158)	Earl of Huntingdon

References

Chapter One

1. Squires and Humphry (1986) pp.68 and 153
2. Cantor (1983) p.3
3. Squires and Jeeves (1994) p.38
4. Ibid. pp.43-48
5. Squires (1996) ch. 2
6. Cantor (1983)
7. Ibid.
8. Cal. Chart. R. 1427-1516 p.242
9. Nichols vol. 3 part 2 p.568
10. Cal. Chart. R. 1427-1516 p.100
11. Harris, John (ed) (1979) p.7
12. See for example Harvey (1981) chapters 4 and 5 and Thacker (1994) chapter 3
13. Ibid.
14. Ibid.
15. LTHAS vol. xix, (1936-37) p.217
16. Ibid. p.216
17. Ibid. p.217
18. Clough (1981) p.8
19. Ibid. p.3
20. Cal Misc. Inquisitions 1377-88 p.161
21. LMVN vol 6, p.111
22. THLAS vol. xiv (1925-26) p.49
23. Ibid p.50
24. THLAS vol xi (1919-20) pp.194-212
25. Fox (1971) p.13
26. Nichols vol. 1, part 2, p.287
27. PRO SC12/23/23. Survey of the Demesne Lands of Bradley Priory.
28. Nichols vol. 3, part 2, p.653
29. LMVN vol 3 p.127
29. Ibid. p.25
30. PRO C135/152/5. Inquisition Post Mortem of Elizabeth de Burgh.
31. Penniston Taylor (1996) p.73
32. LMVN, vol. 6, p.197
33. Most of the section on the Town of Leicester is based on: Bateson (1901) pp.410-450; Thompson (1849); Bilson (1920) pp.1-22 and 123-139
34. 'A True Plan or Ground Plot of the Ancient Corporation of Leicester' by Thomas Roberts, 1741

Chapter Two

1. PRO DL39/2/14. A Perambulation of the King's Forest or Chase of Leicester 1526.
2. BL Add. MSS 38444
3. PRO DL 43/19/6. Survey of the Castle and Forest of Leicester 1524.
4. Fox and Russell (1948) pp.134-35
5. Ibid. p.68
6. Nichols vol. 1, part 2, p.784
7. Cal Pat R. 1549-1551, p.370
8. Nichols vol. 4, part 2, p.781
9. For a history of Donington Park see Squires (1996)
10. VCH(Rut) vol. 2, p.13
11. PRO E178/1246. Valor of the Manor of Ashby-de-la-Zouch 1585.
12. VCH(Leics) vol. 5 pp.266-67
13. PRO. As for reference (1) above.
14. TLHAS vol. xxxii (1956) p.50
15 LRO PP 101. Map of Wistow 1632 and VCH(Leics) vol 3 p.338
16 J. Crocker in pers. com.
17. Hoskins (1963) pp.131-148 although more recently Platt (1978, p.196) and others have recognised the same phenomenon had begun before the close of the middle ages, and extended into the second half of the 17th century.
18. Burton (1622)
19. Toulmin Smith (1964) p.21
20. LRO DG7/1/70. Survey of Burley-on-the-Hill 1657. Also, Finch (1901) vol. 1
21. Pevsner (1960) p.214
22. Nichols vol. 4 part 2, following p.460
23. Nichols vol. 4 part 1 p.110
24. Nichols vol. 3 part 1 p.180 25. THLAS vol. xii (1921-22) p.175; LMVN vol.4 p.92; Ibid. vol.3 p.15

Chapter 3

1. Fleming and Gore (1988) p.50
2. Fearnley-Whittingstall (1993) p.15
3. Oakley (1996) p.31.
4. O'Hagan (1989) p.31

Chapter 4

1. Bilikowska (1983) p.18
2. Woodward (1982) p.24
3. Bowe (1984) p.28
4. Kitchin 1988) p.17
5. Anthony (1979) p.149
6. VCH Rutland (1935) p.86
7. VCH Leicestershire (1964) p.116
8. Carter, Goode and Laurie (1983)

Chapter 5

1. Bilikowska (1983) p.24
2. Hyams (1966) p.71
3. Pevsner (1984) p.138
4. Franklin (1981) p.418
5. Morgan and Richards (1990) p.16
6. Fearnley-Whittingstall 1993 p.19
7. Ibid. p.21
8. Lawrie (1987) pp.212-13
9. Shirley (1867) pp.146-7
10. Whitaker (1892)
11. Pevsner (1984) p.235

Chapter 6

1. Nicolson (1994) p.16
2. Pevsner (1984) p.298
3. Hubbard (1977) p.65
4. Boynton and Pitches (1996) p.84
5. Anthony (1979) p.113
6. Nash and Reeder (1983) p.35
7. Ibid. p.36
8. Fearnley-Whittingstall (1993) p.23
9. Nash and Reeder (1983) p.36

77. *Map of places mentioned in this book*

See also page 12, which has a map of the medieval parks in the two counties, most of which are not duplicated here.

■ Historic Parks and Gardens normally open to the public

● Other places mentioned in the book

Bibliography

Books

Anthony: John Anthony, *The Gardens of Britain, 6: The East Midlands,* Batsford, 1979.

Bateson: M. Bateson (Ed), *Records of the Borough of Leicester 1337-1509,* C. J. Clay, 1901.

Bilikowska: Katrina Bilikowska, *Hampshire's Countryside Heritage: Historic Parks and Gardens,* Hampshire County Council, 1983.

Bilson: Charles James Bilson, *Medieval Leicester,* Edgar Backus, Leicester, 1920.

Bowe: Patrick Bowe, 'Rolling Green Canvas: Capability Brown's Influential Landscapes', *Country Life,* 5 July, 1984.

Boynton and Pitches: Helen Boynton and Grant Pitches, *Domestic Locations, Leicester's Middle Class Suburbs, 1850- 1920,* Leicester City Council, 1996.

Burton: William Burton, *The Description of Leicestershire,* 1622.

Cantor: Leonard Cantor, *The Medieval Parks of England, a Gazetteer,* Loughborough University of Technology, 1983.

Carter, Goode and Laurie: George Carter, Patrick Goode and Kedrun Laurie, *Humphry Repton, Landscape Gardener, 1752-1818,* Victoria and Albert Museum, 1983.

Clough: T. H. McK. Clough, *Oakham Castle, a Guide and History,* Leicestershire Museums Services, 1981.

Farnham: G. F. Farnham, *The Quorndon Records*, Mitchell, Hughes and Clarke, 1912.

Charnwood Forest, Its Historians and the Charnwood Manors, Edgar Backus, 1930

Fearnley-Whittingstall: Jane Fearnley-Whittingstall, *Historic Gardens,* Grange Books, 1993.

Finch: Pearl Finch, *A History of Burley-on-the-Hill,* 1901. Privately printed.

Fleming and Gore: Lawrence Fleming and Alan Gore, *The English Garden,* Spring Books, 1988.

Fox and Percy: Levi Fox and Russell Percy, *Leicester Forest,* Edgar Backus, 1948.

Fox: Levi Fox, *Leicester Abbey,* City of Leicester Publicity Department, 1971.

Franklin: Jill Franklin in G. E. Mingay (Ed.), *The Victorian Countryside, Vol. 2,* Routledge and Kegan Paul, 1981.

Harris: John Harris (Ed), *The Garden,A Celebration of One Thousand Years of British Gardening,* Mitchell Beazeley, 1979.

The Artist and the Country House, Sotherby Parke Barnet, 1978.

Hartley: Robert F Hartley, *The Medieval Earthworks of Rutland,* 1983; *The Medieval Earthworks of North West Leicestershire,* 1984; *The Medieval Earthworks of North East Leicestershire,* 1987; *The Medieval Earthworks of Central Leicestershire,* 1989 (all published by Leicestershire Museums Arts & Records Service)

Harvey: John Harvey, *Medieval Gardens.* Batsford, 1981.

Hastings Manuscripts: *Report on the manuscripts of the late Reginald Rawden Hastings.* HMSO, 1928

Hoskins: W. G. Hoskins, *Provincial England,* Macmillan, 1963.

Hubbard: John R. Hubbard, *Brooksby,* British Agricultural Colleges, 1977.

Hyams: Edward Hyams, *The English Garden,* Thames and Hudson, 1966.

Kitchin: Lawrence Kitchin, 'Ardour in the arbour', *Times Higher Educational Supplement,* 23 September, 1988.

Lawrie: Ian C. Lawrie, *East Cheshire Parks and Gardens,* Sigma Press, 1987.

LMVN: G.F. Farnham, Leicestershire Medieval Village Notes (6 vols.) privately printed, ? – 1933

Morgan and Richards: Joan Morgan and Alison Richards, *A Paradise Out of a Common Field, The Pleasures and Plenty of the Victorian Garden,* Harper and Row. 1990.

Nash and Reeder: David Nash and David Reeder (Eds.), *Leicester in the Twentieth Century,* Leicester City Council, 1983.

Nichols: J. Nichols, *The History and Antiquities of the County of Leicestershire,* 4 volumes, 1795-1811.

Nicolson: Adam Nicolson, 'When an Englishman's home is the nation's castle', *Times Magazine,* 22 October, 1994.

O'Hagan: Mary O'Hagan, *Report on the Evolution of the Park at Burley- on- the- Hill, Rutland,* Unpublished, 1989.

Oakley: Glynn Oakley, *A History of Gopsall,* Barncraft, 1996.

Penniston Taylor: Ralph Penniston Taylor, *Wymondham,* Witeha Press,Wymondham, 1996.

Pevsner: Nikolaus Pevsner, *The Buildings of England, Leicestershire and Rutland,* Penguin, 1984.

Platt: Colin Platt, *The Great Rebuildings of Tudor and Stuart England,* UCL Press, 1994

Potter: T. R. Potter, *The History and Antiquities of Charnwood Forest,* 1842

Shirley: E. P. Shirley, *English Deer Parks,* John Murray, 1867.

Squires and Humphrey: A. E. Squires and W. Humphrey, *The Medieval Parks of Charnwood Forest,* Sycamore Press,Wymondham, Melton Mowbray, 1986.

Squires and Jeeves: Anthony Squires and Michael Jeeves, *Leicestershire and Rutland Woodlands Past and Present,* Kairos Press, 1994.

Squires: Anthony Squires, *Donington Park and the Hastings Connection,* Kairos Press, 1996.

Thatcher: Christopher Thatcher, *The Genius of Gardening,* Weidenfeld and Nicolson, 1994.

Thompson: James Thompson, *History of Leicester to the Seventeenth Century,* 1849.

Toulmin Smith L. Toulmin Smith (Ed.), *The Itnerary of John Leland In Or About the Years 1535-1543,* Centaur Press, 1964.

TLHAS: *Transactions of the Leicestershire Archaeological and Historical Society,* 1886 to Present.

VCH: *Victoria County History — Leicestershire,* Vol. 5, 1964; *Rutland,* Vol. 2, 1935.

Whitaker: John Whitaker, *A Descriptive List of the Deer Parks and Paddocks of England,* Ballantyne, Hanson, 1892.

Woodward: Frank Woodward, *Oxfordshire Parks,* Oxfordshire Museum Services, 1982.

Public Records

BL: *British Library,* London.

Cal. Chart. R. : *Calendar of Charter Rolls,* Public Record Office.

Cal. Close R.: *Calendar of Close Rolls,* PRO

Cal. IPM: *Calendar of Inquisitions Post Mortem*, PRO.

Cal. Misc. Inq.: *Calendar of Inquisitions Miscellaneous,* Public Record Office.

Cal Pat. R.: *Calendar of Patent Rolls,* PRO.

DL: *Duchy of Lancaster Records* in Public Record Office.

LMVN: *Leicestershire Medieval Village Notes,* 6 volumes, Privately Printed, ?-1933.

LRO: *Leicestershire Record Office,* Wigston, Leicester.

Misc. Chancery Inqu.: *Miscelaneous Chancery Inquisitions,* PRO

PRO: *Public Record Office,* London.

Rot. Pat.: *Rotuli Litterarium Patentium,* 1835

INDEX